# Acclaim for *Misgivings*

"A poet's knowing intuition and memory inform this book, which, page by page, turns into a gift of psychological and moral wisdom—a writer's journey toward awareness becomes a reader's responsive experience."
—ROBERT COLES

"The language, like that of all Williams' poems, is hard, crystalline, without frills . . . [*Misgivings* is a] relentlessly honest and blistering memoir . . . a book whose truth is cleansing." —ROBERT LEITER, *Jewish Exponent*

"C. K. Williams's *Misgivings* is a model of decency and honesty. As in his poems, he humanizes here whomever his gaze falls upon, revealing in the process what's most human about us all and what's usually most inaccessible to us . . . It's a beautiful book." —RUSSELL BANKS

"How well the author understands—and communicates throughout—the credulous yearnings of the heart, how in the economy of family life the merest gleam of kindness redeems a hundredweight of bitterness . . . Williams leaves us marveling both at the disastrous rifts and blockages that ruin the promise of connection and the cunning of love, how it ultimately overcomes even these."
—SVEN BIRKERTS, *Ruminator Review*

"Though *Misgivings* is intensely personal, Williams has touched on something universal in the experience of the death of one's parents, something perhaps that only the grace and economy of a great poet could capture."
—DIANE JOHNSON

# C. K. WILLIAMS
## *Misgivings*

C. K. WILLIAMS is the author of eight collections of poems, including *Repair* (1999), winner of the Pulitzer Prize and the *Los Angeles Times* Book Prize. He teaches in the Writing Program at Princeton University and lives part of the year in Paris.

# MISGIVINGS

*My Mother,*

*My Father,*

*Myself*

## C. K. Williams

Farrar, Straus and Giroux
*New York*

Farrar, Straus and Giroux
19 Union Square West, New York 10003

Printed in the United States of America
Published in 2000 by Farrar, Straus and Giroux
First paperback edition, 2001

Library of Congress Cataloging-in-Publication Data
Williams, C. K. (Charles Kenneth), 1936–
  Misgivings : my mother, my father, myself / C. K. Williams. — 1st ed.
    p.    cm.
  ISBN 0-374-52728-8 (pbk.)
  1. Williams, C. K. (Charles Kenneth), 1936—Family.   2. Poets, American—
20th century—Family relationships.   3. Poets, American—20th century—
Biography.   I. Title.

PS3573.I4483 Z47 2000
811'.54—dc21
[B]                                                                99-053290

Designed by Patrice Sheridan

# MISGIVINGS

My father dead, I come into the room where he lies and I say aloud, immediately concerned that he might still be able to hear me, *What a war we had!* To my father's body I say it, still propped up on its pillows, before the men from the funeral home arrive to put him into their horrid zippered green bag to take him away, before his night table is cleared of the empty bottles of pills he wolfed down when he'd finally been allowed to end the indignity of his suffering, and had found the means to do it. Before my mother comes in to lie down beside him.

When my mother dies, I'll say to her, as unexpectedly, knowing as little that I'm going to, "I love you." But to my father, again now, my voice, as though of its own accord, blurts, *What a war!* And I wonder again why I'd say that. It's been years since my father and I raged at each other the way we once did, violently, rancorously, seeming to loathe, despise, detest one another. Years since we'd learned, perhaps from each other, perhaps each in our struggles with ourselves, that conflict didn't have to be as it had been for so long the routine state of affairs between us.

And yet it was "war" that came out of me now, spontaneously, mindlessly, with such velocity I couldn't have stopped it no matter what, but, still, I don't understand why it's this I'd want to say to my father at the outset of his death. As though memory were as wayward and fractious as dream, as indifferent to emotional reasoning, as resistant to bringing forth meanings or truths, verifications that might accord with any reasonable system of values. As though memory had its own procedures of belief and purpose that exist outside of and beyond our vision of our lives.

With my mother, as I remember again now speaking to her in her death, my memory, capricious as ever, brings her to me on the shore of a lake, in a bathing suit. I'm very young—I don't even have a brother or sister yet. My mother is sitting beside me speaking to my father. Bathing suits are made of wool then, even mine, and I'm acutely aware of how rough the fabric must be to my mother's sensitive skin; its abrasiveness is a violation, a desecration: I try to stroke the skin under the straps on her back. My mother smiles at me. My father smiles, too. In the water later, in the shallows, I teach myself to walk on my hands with my body afloat behind me. "Look, I'm swimming!" I cry out in pride to my mother, who, in my memory, breaking off what she was saying then to my father, smiles at me again.

And yet that other spurt of speech from the past, to my father lying before me, as though we'd never effected our unspoken reconciliation, as though we'd never embraced, never, after our decades of combat, held one another, our cheeks touching, our chests for a moment pressed together—to my father come words that seem to contain an eruption of still painful feelings, though I know those feelings have been transformed, transfigured; peace for rage, affection for frustration, devotion and compassion for misunderstanding.

The first time my father and I kissed each other as adults, the first time we managed to move across and through our old enmities, across and through our thousand reservations, our thousand hesitations; the first time we stood that way together, arms around each other, we seemed to me to be uncannily high from the earth: it was as though I were a child again, suddenly stretched to my father's height as I held him, gazing dizzily down in disbelief at the world far beneath us. My mother was there, watching, saying nothing, taken surely at least at that moment with relief for us all, yet too caught in her own timidities and her own travails to dare speak it aloud.

When my father died, it was difficult to comprehend what my mother felt. She threw herself down on the bed next to my father, and lay there quietly for a long time. She said his name several times; she seemed to want to cry, but didn't.

The week before, when she'd first realized he really was going to die, and soon, she'd said, "Now I'll have to go live with all the other widows." She was saying that after he was gone she'd move to a swank apartment house in a nearby town where many of her friends lived. She meant what she said to sound sorrowful, and certainly something like sorrow did bend her voice, but anyone who knew her well would know too that she was excited by the prospect of buying and decorating a new place to live in, of having so much to do, so much to think about.

She had almost cried when my father first started to become aphasic, when his speech deteriorated so that his words were inappropriate or wildly wrong. She must have been frightened that someone who'd lived so much by his gift for language could sound foolish, or mad. Her eyes reddened when she spoke of those first dreadful weeks when the aphasia was manifesting itself, but still, she didn't quite cry. Several years later, in another context, she happened to mention to me how, when my father had their last dog put away, a clumsy, affectionate hound who'd become hopelessly ill, she'd surprised herself, because she'd sobbed like a baby; she couldn't understand why, she said, the dog had been my father's more than hers.

Does my mother not crying when my father died say something about her character, or their marriage, or the fact that my father had long periods over the last decades of his life when he wasn't a very nice man, and that perhaps she'd never come to terms with it?

That's what she'd said to him once, *You used to be such a nice man.* It's what I hear her saying again, perhaps near tears, her voice breaking perhaps in anger or sadness or most likely in surprise at her audacity in speaking aloud what sounded so much like a repudiation. No one will ever know now whether she'd cried, or spoken in a torn or angry or infinitely regretful tone when she said it; she was alone with my father, they're both gone now, and, though she reported to me the words she said to my father, it still seems unlikely that she would have done so, no matter how she said them: it wasn't in her character to share very much that went on between my father and her in their very opaque relationship.

Those were the years of my father's most maddening insensitivity and harshness, when he dealt with all of us, even my mother, as though we were his employees, or worse. He tormented all of us, sometimes by his criticism, by the way he had of letting you know you weren't meeting his expectations, sometimes by his inscrutability and unpredictability—you had no idea from one day to the next how he'd respond to you—and sometimes by his indifference, an indifference which by then had begun to invade his entire character, although he himself wasn't yet suffering from it as he would later. They're the long years, which if I'm not careful can entirely determine my memory of my relation to him, even now, even long after we'd made peace and long after I'd understand at his deathbed how complex that peace was. My mother's remark about his no longer being a nice man ostensibly had to do with how badly my father was dealing with my brother, who'd recently gone to work in one of my father's businesses, but the state of relations between my father and my sister and me and his ever increasing distance from my mother would also have to have been a part of her plaint.

I can imagine my father and mother lying there as my mother speaks. Their bed was very wide, and had been made especially long, because my father was so tall. The fact that it was one bed rather than two implied a union between them, but in those last years, glancing in at them at night when I was visiting and came in late, I never saw them—they always left their bedroom door open—in any sort of contact, bodies wound together or hands touching. They slept back to back; when she spoke those words, my mother might have been facing my father, but I imagine him already turned away from her.

He had to have registered her words, though. If there was a break in her voice, he would have had to be aware of it. Would her distress have caused him to search himself to try to find some justice in what she'd said, would it have made him entertain the least possibility that she might be right, and that he might have to do something about it? Such a grievous accusation to hear from one's own wife. His arms complicatedly folded under his head as they always were when he slept, would he have felt in himself some sadness, some loss, some possible need for repentance or change?

My father had long before sworn that he'd never again say he was sorry, for anything, to anyone. No one ever knew what had brought him to such a resolve, nor did we ever know either what had made him tell my mother about his promise to himself, but she was aware of it, so she would have known not to expect anything like an excuse, or a vow to do better, or any sort of evasion or deflection which could have been interpreted as an apology.

Might he have taken what she said as simply an attack, something in the struggle between them, which might have made her words easier to deflect? My father didn't suffer slights easily; if he thought my mother meant merely to assail him, he'd have slashed back. Would he have allowed her remark to hurt him? Was there still enough feeling in him in those days, enough vital, active, living emotion connecting him to his wife, to any of us, so that what she said would have mattered to him in any deep way? If it had, what then? If he had absorbed her words, and taken into himself what she had said, then he probably would at first have irritably demanded of the void of the night whether she really wanted him to recast the character he'd spent his whole life hammering into existence; "spent" in the sense of paid, paid out, soul and body, conscience and emotion, until he was often in a state of physical and spiritual exhaustion. And what would the night have dared reply?

*This was the room in which my father would die. For me now, anything that ever happened in that room can seem to have already present in it those two events: my mother saying what she did to my father, and his death, the death he would will for himself in that same bed; his death rests off to one side, silent, patient, so that my father as my mother speaks to him seems to be lying alongside himself, and the likelihood of his replying seems as slight as if my mother were speaking to that future ghost.*

*I don't really know if her words hurt him, and yet they hurt me, even now. Whenever they come to mind, they arrive with a shock, of shame, of remorse, as though I had to feel for my father what he was incapable of feeling, or of knowing he was feeling. I can still sense, too, as though I were there with them, how the tiny corner of the night their bedroom contained goes utterly still with my mother's waiting for my father to reply or not reply, and with his deciding whether he will or won't. Or not deciding: it would have to have been something so deep within him that replied that there couldn't have been any actual decision on his part; anything he said would have had to have come out of him spontaneously, without his thinking it first, and he would immediately have had to make clear to both my mother and himself that there was no surrender or submission, even a surrender to whatever in himself had caused him to speak, to be inferred from his response. Submission was an act, a phenomenon, it would have been unthinkable for him to let anyone, even himself, inflict upon him. An upsurging, then, perhaps of a connection long forgotten, long ago put aside so it wouldn't interfere with his crucial interchanges with himself, with the reality he'd shaped to contain those interchanges.*

*Meanwhile, he still hasn't spoken. I can tell even from here how much he would have wanted to be asleep by then; how much he wishes to be left alone. Can he ever be alone again with her there waiting beside him, having said that? Could he bring himself to ask her to explain, or elaborate on what she'd said? "You used to be such a nice man." Certainly it would have needed explication. Certainly he must have been abashed at having his life so compressed, condensed into what was, after all, considering how circumspect my mother normally was with him, a devastating accusation. Yet I can't find in my memory any evidence to show that what she said changed in any way how he acted during those years. I can't imagine either any reply he might have made to her. There's only the silence, and, for me, that image of his death waiting beside him, already beginning to absorb him.*

Perhaps my mother didn't cry when my father died because she was exhausted by all the months of not knowing what was happening to him, then by those last weeks of having to accept that the tumors in his body and his brain were conquering him. It was appalling to behold for all of us, although in the days before his going, when he'd come to terms with knowing he was dying and was only upset because he couldn't convince any of us to help him to get it over with as quickly as possible, he became more gentle, more kind and attentive, solicitous and affectionate, especially to her, than he'd been in many years, and perhaps ever. But my mother, though pleased by his change, still hung back from accepting this near-deathbed transformation, as though she didn't quite believe it.

To me they were very important, those last days. I would chat with my father to try to distract him from his single-minded insistence that someone had to get him whatever pills or injections he needed to kill himself, to end the humiliation his disease was inflicting on him. He had fresh, raw scars on his forearms, the hesitation marks of someone who's tried to do away with himself with a blade; he hadn't been able to do that, but was determined to find another way. You couldn't talk to him for five minutes about anything else without his coming back to suicide, and it wasn't until we told him that someone would, indeed, help him that he would pay attention for more than a few minutes to what you were saying.

Before that happened, though, one afternoon when he was telling me again, yet again, that he wanted me to help him end his ordeal, I tried to change the subject by convincing him that these last days, these last hours we were having together were precious, and that we should try to have as many as we could. As I spoke, tears came to my eyes, my father saw them, his eyes filled, too, and he said, "We were kids together, you and I."

I was very moved; I hadn't seen him in tears for so long. The last time was when I was twenty, when I'd gone away for some months to Europe to try to teach myself to write. I didn't call, wrote few letters, came back on an impulse—I couldn't bear my loneliness any-more—and arrived unannounced. My father wasn't at the house when I got there; my mother of course was glad to see me, but she was in a hurry: she was just leaving to meet my father at a bris, the circumcision service of the son of my father's younger brother, and she took me with her. My father was there when we arrived; he glanced at my mother, then at me, did a sort of double-take, and then the tears came—he had to take off his glasses and use his handkerchief to dry his eyes. Now, this afternoon during the days of his dying, to behold him so taken by a nostalgia for our shared past surprised and gratified me, and I sensed that he wouldn't come to act later as though he regretted his expression of affection, which he still, despite all, occasionally did.

It's true we'd all been young back then, he and my mother and I. My mother and he were both twenty-two when I was born, it was the Depression and they were frighteningly poor—my mother talked even at the end of her life about not having had enough money to buy me an ice cream, and about their slum apartment where she had to stamp her foot when she opened the door so the cockroaches would have time to hide before she turned on the light. There was something about us being poor together—or perhaps for my father it was the novelty of being a husband and father, or it might have been just that he still loved my mother then without qualification—that bound the three of us together in a way the family never quite would be again, except perhaps at parties, when we were a little tipsy and my mother was in her rapture about giving or being part of a celebration, and my father . . .

I don't really know what my father felt even at those times when the rest of us could unbend, and we could be pretty certain for a while, as we never were during his bad times, that he wouldn't strike out at one of us. He was more accessible then, and he was as friendly and warm with us as he was with his friends and business associates, but you still never really knew.

Before the reconciliation he made with me, and with my brother and sister, he could be dreadful, he could be, well, a prick. I've known people who could say something to hurt you, but my father could keep at you, minute by minute, with a disconcerting insistence, as though he had every right to do it, and should immediately be, not forgiven, because he didn't ever find anything at all wrong with what he'd done, but comprehended, given credence, even if the pain he inflicted had been meant to burn, and endure.

For instance, *How's your wife?* he said to me one day, just after I and my then lover who would soon be and still is my second wife had sat down to lunch with him and my mother at their house. It sounds like an innocuous enough question, but it wasn't: he was referring to my first wife, from whom I'd separated a few years earlier and to whom I was still technically married, and he asked the question coldly, as an accusation, a castigation, in a cruel, aggressive tone. I was shocked and embarrassed; I knew that my present wife, who was very sensitive then to anything about my first marriage, would have been vexed by what my father said, but I didn't realize until later how hurt she'd actually been, though she said nothing at the time, to have my father so callously bring up the subject. He knew I was having interminable, tiresome difficulty extricating myself from my marriage, both legally, because my ex-wife was using my wanting to divorce quickly as a way to get some satisfaction of her own, and emotionally, because of our daughter, who was very young, and for whom I felt both guilt and an almost overwhelming need, and what he said was gratuitous, inappropriate, and crude.

"Why don't you ask her?" I answered, which was lame, but, as usual in those days, I was too taken aback when my father did something like that to be able to think quickly enough of a satisfying retort. My father was in a rage at me, but what about? It felt as though he was trying to contaminate the devotion he'd have to have seen I felt toward the woman sitting there with us, and the contentment he must have realized I'd found with her.

Maybe he'd recently spoken to my ex, and believed her recriminations of me, though I was treating her as fairly as I could. Or maybe he was furious at the idea that I'd escaped from an unhappy relationship to begin one that was so fulfilling; surely he'd have thought of doing the same thing during the hard years with my mother, before they'd worked out the truce, or cease-fire or whatever it was they lived with in their last years. Divorce for my parents' generation was rare, but for my father more was involved: it was his conviction that you had to overcome unacceptable impulses and desires, to confront and conquer one's weaknesses every chance you had, and I know he blamed me because I'd taken what he thought was the easy way out.

I never did find out the reason for that particular attack, but he was incensed. He looked at me from under his brows, hard and distant, then turned to his plate and piled it with an absurdly large amount of food, much more than he usually ate. I tried to make peace, saying, "You must be hungry," but he turned that into the excuse for another attack: "What's it to you?"

he answered. Again I was speechless. That grotesque mound of food he meant, too, as an indictment, of what I still didn't know, but its presence in front of him seemed to keep his rage resonating all the time he was jaggedly forking it into himself; he ate every bit.

As I say, my father really could be a prick. He once came to a business convention in the city where I was living and invited me to lunch. Coming out of the meeting center, I was trailing a little behind him and saw a group of other men look over at him—he didn't see them—and one of them gave him the finger, violently, with evident rage, as though the man had personally been cheated or betrayed by my father. I'm sure my father had many business enemies; if you're successful in as grindingly competitive a business as his, there must be many opportunities to be . . . dreadful; but I was taken aback by the sheer malice of the stranger's gesture: it implied more than just hard trade tactics.

My father *had* been a nice man, especially when I was young, although I suppose most people think that about their father: the father you have defines at least at first what the possible limits of fatherly intimacy are, doesn't he? Mine was loving with me, thoughtful, always teaching me little things—I remember him showing me once how miraculous our skin was, how it shed water so well, how when it was stretched it returned to its shape, and he explained how it kept replacing itself all our lives. He used to take me with him on Sunday mornings when he went to play softball, and I reveled in watching him; he was a good athlete and always hit the ball farther than anyone else. If someone did make a hit longer than his, I'd be affronted by the disrupted order of things.

There's the other part of being a child, too, of course: I can remember him coming home from work and my mother reporting to him some misbehavior for which she felt I hadn't been adequately punished—(*Just wait till your father gets home*)—and him standing in the doorway of my bedroom, his belt in his hand, his other hand gesturing me to go by him so he could . . . I don't know what the word would be, "whip" me, I suppose, but that's an overstatement. Really he'd just swipe me across the behind, and probably not very hard; there was certainly nothing like what they now call "abuse." The only times I can remember him hitting me hard was when I'd do something outrageously stupid: once we were in a park, there was a big puddle he'd specifically warned me to stay away from, and I still managed somehow to fall into it and cover myself with mud. He dragged me back to the car, saying nothing, but I could tell he was furious. How grinding those moments between realizing that you're going definitely to be punished and the punishment itself. In the car, he smacked me on my behind, hard enough so this time it really did hurt, and I cried all the way home, him never looking at me nor saying a word.

But no matter the degree of pain those few times he hit me, his anger was worse; just knowing he was angry made me cry helplessly; but he'd always soon come to take me in his arms, and no matter how hurt or frightened I was, I'd be solaced.

How many times did he actually physically hurt me? I don't know. At least that once or twice; enough, surely, for me to still remember it; not often enough so that the love I had for him then, my absolute absorption in him, was ever jeopardized.

*I'm speaking of my parents as though they were emblematic of something, as though there were some aura of meaning about them that transcended the small stories—and I realize they are small stories—that contain them. At the beginning, and for a long while after, our parents are all like that, of course, the heroes of our lives as well as their own: their very being defines the dimension of our existence for us, and embodies the realities that express that existence. And surely all of that stays somewhere in our psyches, and in the selves we live out every day; we need that vision perhaps more than we like to admit, and we have a much more reflexive compulsion to refer to it than we let on; even after we're well socketed in our own lives, how often do we use that ancient scale to situate ourselves against, to check our truths against, as we check countless times whether our notion of our own magnitude is justified?*

*I'm aware that my father was an ordinary businessman, like thousands of others, and that my mother was a perfectly typical housewife of her time and place, first in a meager financial situation, then quite well-off. She'd been very pretty when she was young, and was always slim and vivacious enough for us to believe she still was, but she was hardly a movie star. My father, as I've said, was very tall, and people found him imposing: when I was a child it was impossible not to see him as different from the rest of the world, as having a unique grandeur that simply wasn't evident in anyone else; I beheld him and I think he thought of and presented himself as indeed symbolic of some special dimension of reality. But, again, doesn't everyone have to have such distortions or illusions to help carry us forward into our lives? We know we give up our mismeasures, that we have to—mostly we hardly notice we're doing it—we shift our infatuation for the symbolic and emblematic to others, usually to figures we don't actually know, those who are famous, or notorious, and about whom it always seems urgent we know more, possess more, more images, more absurd fancies; the farther we are from them, the more we magnify their magnificence, the more we crave even the most vicarious connection with them. And yet all that older, more real sense of magnificence stays within us, too, attached to the primitive vividness of those still shining within us, who once dominated everything else, and made such radical discrepancies between our scale and everything else seem the rightful order of things.*

*We see our early lives so much as though through a lens that bends all the light of existence toward that tiny circle in the center of which we pose for ourselves. When we look at ourselves, though, and at those others once so near, as we're cast against the shadows of the reality of the larger world that contains everything, that chaotic, unlikely screed of possibility and dread, we find we're constantly rearranging the group portrait of our contemplation, because nothing in it can ever remain quite as it was even a moment ago. Yet doesn't all we've gone through have a domain where it persists always just as it once was? Though every minute we live can make its own demands,*

*require its own justifications, its own healing, aren't there al-
ways still those covert images and feelings, even odors and
tastes, out of which we began and which will always assert
their essential linkage to everything else, every other emotion,
every fugitive or fleeting speculation as to who we might finally
be?*

I can think sentimentally of those years when our family was poor, and perhaps my father could, too, but my mother never did; for one thing, beside her frustrated desires, our being so close to going hungry had to have generated problems between her and my father. I remember arguments about money, more than a few, but at least in those days that's what the conflicts were really about; the reason they fought about money wasn't because it stood for feelings which could no longer be articulated, the way it happens in so many marriages, and later on in theirs, too: in those days money fights had to do with real issues, with figuring out ways to get what they needed to live, not with everything else.

When things did get better, my mother was always actively thankful not to be poor anymore; she never stopped relishing having the wherewithal to be able to do and possess what she wanted. Those years of need remained with her as a rankling norm, a state against which everything else had to be measured, a condition to which one might return at any moment, and which had to be referred to before anything could happen. All her life, when she had the chance to buy something, she'd become elated; it was as though she was having revenge on those wasted years when there was hardly enough to get by, not to speak of money to spend on anything not absolutely essential.

So the purchase of her first fur, "Persian lamb" coat had about it the mystic charge of a hermetic initiation ritual; conferences with her sister and friends about the kind of fur and the color, trips to this or that furrier until she found one who'd offer both quality and style and enough of a discount so she could feel she was getting a bargain. Then at last a dramatic appearance in the living room before the family, her hand in a pocket, her collar rakishly up in back, her torso half turned away from us, her feet in that ballet position women like to use when they're posing. We were all very happy for her, and shared in her rejoicing. But even when she had her fur coat, her Studebaker, her charge accounts, she fretted; it was a long time before she could believe we were well enough off so she could feel more than relatively secure.

Many businessmen in my father's postwar generation succeeded, but my father started doing well earlier than many, so when he first had some extra money there weren't many others who did yet, and if my parents weren't in any sense among the real rich, they could occasionally live as though they were. Soon after we moved to the suburbs, my mother wanted to hire the wife of a couple who worked as maid and butler-chauffeur for some very wealthy people they knew who were moving away. My father had no need for and couldn't afford either a chauffeur or a butler, but he satisfied my mother's fancy for a domestic coup by offering the husband a job driving a truck. The man was delighted; he'd spent his whole adult life working with his wife and couldn't have been more pleased to be on his own for a change. He was a good worker, a pleasant and intelligent person, and my father and he became very much chums.

I think many of my father's most satisfying relationships were with people who worked for him. There was another employee whose life my father changed significantly and who became very attached to him; a man, in his early thirties I'd guess, who'd started out working in the main business as a repairman. I never cared for him much: his eyes had a way of seeming reluctant to meet yours and he had the narrow face and sallow complexion of a kid I knew in grammar school who'd been held back so many times that he was sixteen when the rest of us were ten, and who even then had a palpable sense of defeat and failure about him. My father, anyway, had decided that the repairman would make a good salesman, trained him himself, and the man did indeed turn out to be one of the best my father ever had. The two of them became very close; sometimes I'd be jealous; it was clear that my father enjoyed spending time with him more than with any of us. When the man died suddenly during supposedly routine surgery, although my father didn't speak much about it, his shock was palpable, and I always felt he was more moved by that death than any other.

The ex-chauffeur's relationship with my father ended badly. He'd been driving trucks for some years when he had a heart attack on the job. He survived, but his old employer, who was a lawyer, convinced him to sue my father because my father knew, or should have known, that he had a heart condition and oughtn't to have been doing heavy work. My father was enraged, and perhaps wounded, though he never let anyone see him taken by something so unmanly as hurt feelings. He won the suit, at any rate, and the ex-chauffeur quit or retired, though his wife, unconcerned by it all, stayed on with my parents a few more years before retiring herself.

*I'm in a room with my mother. I'm looking not up but straight across at her, so I must be standing, perhaps in a crib. My mother is next to a window; I watch her, though she doesn't know that I do. A block of yellow sunlight fills part of the room, and when it touches my mother—she's naked, or partly naked—it turns gold, and then the whole room is glowingly golden. I'm acutely aware of my mother's body, especially her breasts; surely I've seen her breasts before—she nursed me for some weeks—but never with the appalled half-furtiveness with which I behold them now: I seemed to have experienced beauty and shyness and shame all in the same intake of breath.*

*Perhaps, too, this is the first realization I have that my mother and I are no longer an entity, a single thing, because I'm conscious all at once that her body consists of separate parts, her breasts, her face, her arms lifted over her head, and that to register these parts my eyes have to move from one position in space to another, each move defining a certain distance, a distance from her I've never experienced before. Her eyes I can tell are looking abstractedly down out of the window; her arms lifted that way means that she must have been combing her hair; I somehow know already how she cherishes her lovely red hair.*

When you'd call her and ask how she was,
if things weren't going well, my mother
would always say, *Pretty good.* Unless she
answered, "Great," or "Terrific," you knew
you had to say next, "What's wrong?" Even
at the very end of her life, when she was
mortally ill, that's still what she'd say, *Pretty
good,* but we all knew then to leave it at
that.

Her stoicism, though, had definite
boundaries. It seemed to be limited mainly
to us, her children, and mostly to her first
response, that greeting which carried the
essential news that she was bearing up, no
matter what her tribulation of the moment. After that, if she felt it was appropriate for her to go on with her complaints or
questionings, she was good at that, too.
When she was first told she had terminal
lung cancer (though no one dared to put it
to her that way) she said, "Sure, I smoked,
but so did all my friends, and they don't
have lung cancer." She was genuinely indignant. What could I say? I used to
smoke, I could imagine the regret she must
have been feeling.

Still, on the whole she took her last

illness and even her dying very well; there was something noble about her self-possession those last months. You wouldn't have said that often about her before, but even at the very worst, even in the last week before she died, she kept her composure and her dignity. She called me one night that week to ask if I was going to rent a car or whether she should pick us up when we came to visit her. My wife and I were supposed to go see her a month later; I thought it odd that she'd want to know so far ahead about our plans. I told her I'd rent a car, then asked, "How are you doing?" "Pretty good," she said. I learned later that she'd gone for a scan that day and that the doctor had told her there was nothing more he could do for her, that she just had to go home now to wait to die, but she never said a word about all that.

I don't know how our family evolved that particular locution for my mother to use. "Pretty good" had become almost a joke by the time of her dying, and we could even laugh about it with her. *Of course we all know you're not well,* we'd be saying, *this is a convention which gives us—what?—some distance perhaps, some place to stand where what's happening to you won't be quite so dire, and it'll also allow us some strands of words to speak that won't imply sad finalities.* I laughed that night on the phone the last time she said it to me, and she did, too. Three days later, on the way home from the movies with some friends, she had trouble walking, then back at her apartment she became irrational, not recognizing the woman who'd been taking care of her, demanding that she leave, then falling shortly afterwards into the coma from which she never emerged.

But even as she lay there unconscious, there was a kind of deflection from the inevitable, a "pretty good." When she first went into the hospice where she'd die, the doctor there said she'd be gone in twenty-four hours; three days later, she was still breathing, on and on, her open mouth biting for one more bulb of air, her color fading, her body despite the medications sometimes convulsing. My brother and sister and I and our spouses were there, and my daughter and her husband; there were relatives in the area who'd drop in, and her being in that dreadful coma and taking so long to die was wearing us all down. At last, on the fourth morning, the hospice nurse told us there were indications of impending death: my mother's feet and hands were growing cooler, and she was becoming white, especially around the mouth, a sure sign; despite our grief, we were relieved. Then that afternoon my aunt, my mother's sister, who had always been her best friend, came to sit with her. Four or five of us were in the room, talking in low voices about how long it was still taking, and my aunt suddenly exclaimed loudly to my mother, *Go already, can't you see you're driving everybody crazy?* She and my mother had always loved one another, though certainly they'd argued over the course of their life, and now, as though they were having another of their little disputes, my mother rallied, her color improved, her temperature rose. The nurse couldn't understand it, everyone found it amusing, but, really, we were at the end of our strength. The next morning I decided my family and I should fly home to wait there, and of course it was then that the call came saying it was over.

*My father refused to wait for his death to come for him; to keep him a few days more we had to implore him to not take himself from us. With my mother, how it went on. Several times during those long days, my wife and I left the hospice and drove a few miles down a horrid strip of malls and gas stations to a beach. There was an old-fashioned wooden structure with an open platform jutting out over the water, and hundreds of seagulls circled in front of it waiting for handouts. Once we brought some bread and spent a while feeding them. A sharp breeze was blowing, and the gulls would hang in the air almost unmoving a few yards away, wonderfully dipping and swaying to stay in place, and when we'd hold out a chunk of bread they'd lunge in to snatch it from our hands or, if we let a piece fall, they'd catch it in mid-flight, then bank gracefully away out over the roaring waves.*

*I was so tired by then I felt that the backs of my eyes had generated receptors whose only function was to ache with fatigue, and it was luxurious to let my gaze sweep out after the gulls rather than being attached as it had been for so long to my mother's reluctantly relinquishing mortality.*

My mother and I, my mother and father and I, so much complexity, so much of what had been happiness become anguish, before it could become something else. Once, my father said to me, quietly, not unpleasantly, quite cordially in fact, coolly, in a tone as though he were complimenting me, *You're a bastard, just like your mother.* I'd almost rather not tell where we were when he said it; it makes an already embarrassing confession even more so. If I'm going to relate anything, though, about my father and mother and myself, how can I not record his pulverizing crack? It was at my brother's wedding, his first, in a suite in a hotel. My father and I were standing next to each other in the first row of the rather cramped space where the ceremony was taking place. My brother and his bride had just been declared man and wife, they began to kiss, and kept on kissing, in a long, cinematic clinch, which went on quite a bit longer than such things usually do, and my father reached out and grabbed my brother's arm, saying something like, "That's enough." He was smiling, but one felt there was as much impatience, or offended propriety in his seemingly good-humored gesture, and, trying to untangle the awkwardness of the moment, I said something like "They're okay, Dad"; I don't remember my words having anything more pointed about them that might explain my father responding the way he did

*A bastard like your mother.* Was what he said as charged with malice as I thought? The word "bastard" isn't all that strong, but wouldn't it have been devastating right then, right there, in a makeshift synagogue, with a hundred people standing behind us, watching us, surely wondering what my father had said? And what a wide arc of destruction: my mother and I, both objects of rancor and contempt in my father's eyes. I had never imagined I could be contemptible to him: that was appalling, but that my mother could be characterized the same way, as a bastard along with me, was a double affront.

I can't remember the rest of the party, it was a long time ago, but I must have resonated through the whole thing with my father's enmity, his ill will, his cold, impassive intonation. What was he telling me? That both my mother and I were insensitive to his feelings, that we valued social formulae more than his sensitivities, so that he no longer considered us to be in an essential union with him? Why might he think my mother and I had become aligned in collusion against him? That would have been hard for me to believe: I was much more attached to him than I was to her then, I probably always had been.

The statement implied a past, too: the force of his accusation wouldn't have resulted from any single act,

one single error or offense on my part. He was imply-
ing that my mother and I had each already attained the
category of bastard, that what I had said was merely
corroboration. Yet when had that happened? When had
my mother and I become so distressingly blameworthy?
I don't remember whether my mother heard his remark: by this time in her life she'd come to conceal
most of her feelings about my father anyway. I think
the two of them had worked out that agreement, I assume unspoken, which would last the rest of their lives,
whereby the mildly unpleasant, inconvenient, irritating,
could be uttered by my mother, but nothing beyond; as
for my father, he never said anything to insult my
mother (unless she'd heard this now), but neither would
he evidence real affection for her, except, rarely, when
they were with other people, in circumstances where
the symptoms of agreeable intimacy were conventions
anyway. So, watching them dancing at a party, you'd
think they were an ideal couple, both smiling, both apparently delighted to dip and swirl with such an attractive and experienced partner.

I remember them dancing like that at their fiftieth
wedding anniversary party: everyone's watching them,
they both look dashing. My mother has on a beautiful
new dress, and she's beaming with pleasure, as though
my father had just wonderfully surprised her with some
new step, and my father looks, unless you'd known him
before, healthy, physically impressive, tanned, graceful.
Six months later, though, he'd be dead, his cancer having spread all over his skeleton and into his brain. Even
their dancing that night was deceptive: my father's
knees by then were so worn out with osteoarthritis that

he could barely walk, and he moved with a pronounced limp, although when he danced the awkwardness in his gait disappeared. The same sort of thing happened at the end with his aphasia: when he'd be talking about anything but business the wrong words would come— "Get me out of this hotel," he'd said to me in the hospital when the tumors were first discovered under his skull—or no words at all, but when he spoke to my brother or one of his managers about business, everything would be fine: no mistakes, nothing he wanted to say couldn't be said.

I cherish the image of them dancing that night, though I know the illusions it contains. The identity of a contentedly loving couple, even if it was assumed, fit them well. They did look the part; my mother's gaiety, my father's pride in how striking they were, he so tall, and she still so pretty. He even looked at her when they danced, which I don't remember his doing very often by then. I'd imagine they'd have danced the same way back then at my brother's wedding, too, while I watched, submerged in my humiliation and shame.

*All the living souls, Theseus, Orpheus, Aeneas, Dante, who've descended into death: is it always this difficult? As though you had to lift your loved ones and carry them out physically, as though from a burning city, to bring them back to where you can really see and be with them again, to understand them and yourself? And they seem to want to make it as difficult for you as they can: it's as though they contrive even to weigh more; I feel as if my father hanging from my shoulders, and my mother, from his, have purposefully increased their density so that I have to feel each atom of the mass of their reluctance to do this with me.*

*To go down into the shadows, down among the shades; how faint these lives can be, how cries of regret can seem indistinguishable from sobs of relief, and how hard to tell if mouths are grimacing in pain or smiling in encouragement. How faint one's own life, too, this close to the dead, how much one's own reality seems to fade in and out of certainty, and consequence.*

*At the end, all one really knows is what all who go down into that world know, that the most miserable hour on earth is better than these freezing glades that deny sensation and repentance, deny all but gropings through the matter of forgetfulness, the prisms of what is eternally gone behind us.*

My father's oath never to say he was
sorry: what does it mean when you decide
you'll never again, to anyone, even to your
wife, even to any of your children, apologize, about anything? Is it an ethical decision? Something that comes out of a
long consideration of moral necessities
and imponderables? Is it the logical conclusion of one's vision of a cosmos which
includes self, beyond-self, other selves, and
a God, or some semblance of a God? And
how does one arrive at a conclusion so co-
herent and compelling that anything else
seems a positive affront to your belief
system?

Or is making such a decision, a resolution of such inclusiveness, more of a psychological realization? The perception that
when one wounds or offends someone
else, there's already pain in having to admit
that you have, and an apology would only
add to the total quotient of misery between offender and offended?

Or does it have something to do with
the sense of one's self-making, with coming to believe that self-creation isn't a con-
tinuing, indeterminate process, but that it
has an end, comes to fruition and stops;

that one can, must say, "I'm finished, the identity I have evolved is no longer open to negotiation, change is no longer an option"? And then one would have to infer that apology would imply just such potential change, imply an "improvement" to one's character, or at least to the past of one's character, because apologies of necessity are made first facing backward into the past; the acceptance of the apology presumably then gives permission for a turn again toward the future, which one may move toward again with a cleansed conscience and no residue of guilt. If one believes, though, that one has completed oneself, that there's no longer any necessity to consider change, culpability becomes something that will always remain safely in one's past, an unfortunate misstep or misunderstanding or misintention that has no living connection to the future, and only incidentally to the present.

But still, how not appear to oneself as insufferably narcissistic and arrogant in arriving at such a resolution? How not sound as though one has defined oneself as a kind of emotional aristocrat, for what could be more imperious than believing one has the right to such dominion, even over oneself? The answer might be that one resolves such quandaries by deciding at the same time that one will never mention one's resolve, because announcing that one will never again apologize would be tantamount to asking for pardon in advance for anything one might do, thereby effecting a tempering, a narrowing, almost an actual negation of one's resolution before one has even had a chance to enact it.

My father once sold one of his businesses to someone he knew slightly. A year or so later, the business began to lose money, and the person who bought it spread the word among his friends, some of whom knew my father, that my father had cheated him. I never found out the actual details, but in the eyes of some people, including, strangely enough, a rabbi who was my father's friend and to whom he'd once given a car, my father's integrity was called into question. He never said a word about any of it. He never explained to anyone his side of what had happened—that might have been the prelude to an apology—and he certainly never said, even to the rabbi, he was sorry.

Later, it turned out that the purchaser of the business had made a bookkeeping error and had to admit that he'd been wrong, that my father in fact had dealt fairly with him. At my father's funeral service, the rabbi used that story as an example of my father's noble reticence, of his worthiness and uprightness.

Good. Splendid. A *mensch* who acts like a mensch. How argue with that? And yet . . . What if the repercussions of the silence after an act are more intricate than those in a commercial transaction? What if at stake is a wound inflicted on someone who loves you, a son, or a daughter, or a wife, whom you've unthinkingly, or heedlessly, or with insufficient sensitivity—or, you wouldn't have even had to know why, with actual cruelty—misused, harrowed, maligned? What if the person you've treated so badly has no idea where your ill feeling might have come from, so that you've really inflicted two cruelties: one overt, the other covert, which leave the one injured trying to find in his own actions, in his own moral identity, the grounds for having brought so much ill-feeling into effect?

Aren't you making a kind of challenge to the other? Aren't you saying: Can you dare not love me, can you dare turn from me with a resolve equivalent to the resolve which determines my reticence? I am ready to risk, aren't you saying, the love I might feel for you and the love you might enjoy, or need from me; I am ready to gamble it all for the sake of my silence, for the sake of that which I believe in the deepest sense defines me, and thus all my relationships, even with those closest to me?

How is the other, the one wounded, to defend against such a position? Can that other say to you: tell me something, tell me *anything* that might explain your cruelty or your apparent refusal to believe in my capacity to be hurt. Wouldn't such a plea be a devastating negation of what the other might have arrived at in his own complex of self-making, even a self-making that has no intention ever to declare itself so accomplished as to be a fortification from which to look out into the world?

And then, even if no such plea has been made, it would have to be implicit in however the one attacked manifested the pain of that attack: with a flinch, a stricken inarticulateness, with the subtlest shutting down or choking off of the flow that evidences itself every instant between two human beings facing one another. Even if no plea were made, wouldn't even more despondency be generated?

*I'm nine years old, away from home alone for the first time, at summer camp. I'm very happy there; I like being with the other kids day and night, I like our little responsibilities, making our beds, sweeping out the cabins, clearing weeds from the fields. I sometimes take walks by myself into the mysterious woods, which frighten me because of how complex and unknowable they are, but I'm pleased, too, to be able to confront and vanquish my timidity.*

*It's the first visiting day. I haven't seen my mother and father for three weeks, which has never happened before; I don't feel I miss them—the only time I think of them is when I write the postcard we have to send out every day. Now, this afternoon, we're being led down the dirt road to the area near the dining hall where we're going to meet our parents. I'm talking with one of my friends, when suddenly I see my mother and father walking up the road and to my surprise I find I've begun to run toward them. They're standing a few feet apart—how suddenly wrenching it is to see them again—and as I approach them I start to swerve from a trajectory that would take me to my mother, to another that would lead to my father. It's indelible in me, that swerving, the inertia of the force of my speed pulling at me as I try to decide to whom to run first, into whose embrace first be taken. My parents are both amused, because they can see my quandary; and they're pleased, too, I imagine, that I'm so ingenuously eager to see them.*

*I don't remember, strangely enough, into whose arms I arrived. I can't even make myself guess. I know how my mother would have reached down, putting her head next to mine, letting me feel her warmth, the circle of her arms around me; and I can feel my father lifting me and swinging me over his head, high, into that luminous firmament to which only he had access.*

Sometimes I feel I'm still swerving between my father and mother the way I did that day. The stakes seem to be more serious now, though I don't know quite why I would think so. Perhaps because trying to relive that moment of indecision again, I realize I'd have gone into the arms of the one I thought would be most slighted that I'd chosen the other; perhaps I still would. I know that I already sensed things like that then; I already know that the space between my parents has implications of the heart, not merely of where and how they might be standing, I'm already conscious of a division between them, and that across the abyss of that division lie many incipient sadnesses and resentments. Even now, I keep wanting to be sure I'm doing both of them justice, not favoring one or the other. I suppose my father takes up more space here, as he did in my life. Physically, of course, he did take up more room, more palpable reality than my mother: he bulked, he *loomed* in a way she never did; his sheer volume must have been nearly double hers.

But certainly I should be speaking of

emotional and spiritual rather than spatial matters. There's no question my mother, as mothers are assumed to be, seemed limitlessly available for me when I was young. Scrapes and sorrows too trivial for my father to bother with would send me rushing to her presence, a presence which would absorb me and hold me for however much time reality had to be suspended so I could deal with it again. She gave me her time and attention without stint and without question during those first years, if only perhaps, I can't help thinking, because she was still too poor to afford many other distractions. By the time my brother and sister were born, our financial situation was a little, then a lot better, and my mother would go out in the afternoon to play mahjong or canasta, and at night with my father to restaurants and parties, leaving us with sitters. When I was young, there was no question of sitters; she had to take me with her, maybe she still wanted to take me with her: we'd go to department stores, where she must have spent as much time wishfully wandering as shopping, or to parks, which were escapes from the cramped rooms we lived in, and sometimes even back to my parents' home town, to her mother's place, where my father had to send us sometimes because he wasn't earning enough to feed all three of us. I remember waiting on the train platform with her as a colossal, shrieking, saurian gray locomotive came toward us, and how, though I was too stunned to speak, she held me tightly to her because she could tell I was frightened even without my telling her. When we were at her mother's she'd sometimes take me out for a "soda pop," or a "frappé," both exotic to me because the words for them were different in the city where we lived with my father.

Then, I don't know for certain when, she was lost to me, not in the way mothers have to be lost as their offspring begin to come into their own lives, but because there was too much else that occupied her. When I was barely four, she took me to the local school to try to have me admitted to kindergarten a year earlier than I normally should have been. I guessed that she wanted me to go to school so she could have relief from the responsibility of taking care of me, but she'd formulated her wish as a compliment: I was to attend school because I was too smart not to; I was only technically, not intellectually, too young. I was very eager to please her, even if pleasing her meant being without her, and I pretended to be as happy as she was when I was accepted.

"Give," says my father, demanding the reins of my horse.

I have a horse. Astonishing. I have a horse of my own. Though I'm told she's not only mine, she's my brother's, too, I know better: he's too young. It's me who wakes at dawn on weekends and hitchhikes up to spend the day at the stable, brushing and feeding her, riding her and cooling her out, who sometimes sneaks up after school or even cuts classes to be with her. A horse of my own. For two or three years, every day, it must have seemed every minute, I've begged my father to buy me one. I'm obsessed by horses. I spend all my free time at livery stables, shoveling manure, shaking out straw and hay, and walking kids on ponies so I can take a ride for a few minutes at the end of the afternoon as my pay. As soon as I have five dollars I spend it on riding. I've read every book on horses and horse people in every library in the city. Finally, partly because my father must realize my passion is serious, and partly because he's found someone he can trust, the brother-in-law of a friend, who has a stable and will keep an eye on me, and who's a

Jew besides, which makes my having a horse more within the realm of the socially imaginable, he buys one. I don't care how or why I get the horse, though: I have her. A spotted mare, cold-blooded, of no distinction whatsoever—she cost a hundred dollars—I'm completely taken with her, mad for her, with everything about her, the oats she eats, the straw in the bottom of her stall, even the bare ground in front of the stable with hoof prints in it, the grass in the pasture, the manure in the grass. I fuss constantly, grooming her, oiling her saddle, and the tangle of straps and the gleaming metal of her bridle.

All the time I've had my horse, my father has never given any indication he's ever been on one, or ever wanted to be, but this afternoon when he's come by the stable to pick me up and has watched me ride for a while, he says he wants to ride himself. I'm horrified. My horse is so small, for one thing—I'm almost too tall for her myself—and he's huge; he's six seven and must weigh then at least two hundred and forty pounds. He must know he's too big for her. Also, she's a little erratic, given to abrupt, unpredictable veerings, toward the fence where I tether her, toward the field where she grazes at night. Sometimes I can barely hang on to her myself, and I'm a good rider. Why do you want to ride? I ask.

My father doesn't bother to explain, he just says again, quite harshly now, "Give," and I know I have to hand him the reins, lengthen the stirrups—they still aren't really long enough—and hold the horse while he awkwardly mounts. He looks absurd on her. Not just that his feet hang down well below her belly, nor that he doesn't know how to hold the reins or position his torso; he perpetrates a much more active aesthetic violation. He and she: the angles are all wrong, the lines, the shapes of the ideal I keep so much in mind when I'm on the horse myself. I'm what's called a "shadow rider," so taken with the image of myself and the horse that I'm given to watching our shadow flowing along on the ground beside us.

My father on my horse, then, is involved in, causes, an aesthetic offense so deformed, so close to the grotesque, so far from the prefigured image my mind has modeled of a man on a horse, and of my father doing anything, that all my sensitivities, my standards of propriety, are violated, and I feel that a moral offense, a profanation, is being committed. All the reality containing such a disfigurement is suspended; it wants only to reject this, to purify itself of this. The memory in my mind is still so dense. I remember what my father was wearing—a tan rain jacket, brown pants—and, again, how unseemly he looked: I can still see the way his hands were held too high and too wide apart, how his legs bulkily and gracelessly dangled; I imagined that my horse's spine would be crushed under his weight.

He only rode for a few minutes; the horse was very nervous, and he must have felt it. Holding the reins while he dismounted, I was relieved, but still confused and upset. Why had he insisted on riding my horse in the first place? He must have known he wasn't going to enjoy it. Was it just a whim? At the time I may have thought what he wanted was to share my horse obsession with me. My pleasures must have been so evident to him, he had to have perceived the joy with which I left to hitchhike the long miles to the stable—he'd have known I'd have walked if I'd had to, or crawled. Even long after when there were no longer horses in my life, when I'd stopped riding and stopped even consciously thinking about it, involved first with girls and sex then with writing, the sight of a horse in a field or trotting by the side of a road, even the smell of a plug pulling a wagon or a policeman's horse could take me back to that world. Might my father have wanted to glean an inkling of my joy?

I don't think so. All this happened at the time when he was just beginning to be arbitrarily severe with us, and I've come to be convinced that what he was doing that perplexing afternoon was making certain I understood that what I thought was my possession really wasn't: he was telling me that he participated in that possession, that in fact he defined it, that I'd better understand that because he had paid for the horse, she ultimately belonged to him. And furthermore, he was asserting himself not only over my possession of the horse but over the entire range of my new imagination, a vision of reality which I'd been foolish enough to think I could partake of without reference to him: in a sense he was taking my horse back.

I think I must have registered what he was doing that day even if I couldn't articulate it to myself. If I feel resentment even now, though, it's not only because of his imperiousness, but as much because it was the first time he'd revealed to me that there could be such a discrepancy between our visions of life, such a contradiction between our notions of rightness. By the time he announced a few years later that the horse had to be sold because he couldn't afford her upkeep anymore, which I knew wasn't true, I must not have greatly cared; I hardly protested, but there was still something that remained, rankling me. Watching from the back of my mother's car as the horse was carted away in a trailer, I almost cried, and I knew I would have if my mother hadn't been watching me with an expression of something like pity—I knew it was probably she who'd insisted on getting rid of the horse; she'd never really accepted my doing something none of her friends' children did, so I would have been indignant to have acknowledged her compassion—but beyond that, I hated feeling that she and my father had conspired against me.

When I picture my father on my horse, in-
elegant and graceless, it comes to me to
think of him in a car as well, because there
he was another person entirely. The period
in which I can most readily imagine him
behind the wheel is when I was in high
school, on one of those rare days when
he'd drop me off on the way to work: usually he'd be gone before I had breakfast,
and I'd hitchhike. Even on those mornings
when I do catch him, though, I have to
rush because he always has an early appointment and might leave without me, so
I run out to the car, and a moment later
we're heading the few miles down the hills
of our town to the school. My father is
wearing a suit and the business hat he still
sported in those days, and he drives with a
deft, athletic, unselfconscious ease. As he
does, he peels an orange—his breakfast—
manipulating the steering wheel with the
delicate pressure against it of one slightly
raised knee; the fingers of his right hand
curve and without him looking at the fruit
his nails insert themselves into the skin at
precisely the most efficacious point for it
to be cleanly stripped, then he throws out

the peels and segments the orange, one section at a time going neatly into his mouth. He always offers me a slice, but I rarely take it, not because I've had my breakfast—I'm always hungry in those days—but because I'm fascinated by his ritual, and with how he can drive so skillfully while apparently paying no attention. Late in his life, because of his deteriorating eyesight, he had several accidents and became very nervous when he drove, jerking the wheel and slamming on the brakes unnecessarily; it was terribly upsetting to watch.

The other thing that intrigued me on those school mornings was how quickly his mind would go away from me; by the time we were a block from our house he'd already be in his business mind, his "real" mind I'd say now, although I wouldn't be able to pinpoint when I began to understand, to acknowledge, to submit to knowing that his working hours were the defining essence of his day, and his life, that they preceded in importance everything else, including the family's relations with him, and his attention or lack of attention to those relations. I did feel, I'm sure, at least an inchoate rebellion, a barely contained resistance to that inviolable, irrevocable position at which he'd arrived. Would he have known entirely that he was making that choice, a choice which would turn him into a not nice man, a man, moreover, who wouldn't have cared whether anyone on earth thought he was or wasn't nice? It's impossible to imagine him not knowing all this, just as it's impossible to think of him not having decided to fashion himself as he was. There was always a force to his demeanor that seemed to announce that everything about him had been willed—every act, every feeling, even the moments he allowed himself of so-called re-laxation seemed to be stages in the progress of that will.

Cars were very much a part of our doings with one another then, going somewhere in a car, thinking about buying or repairing a car. In my father's last years, when he became bored with almost everything in his life, even, at last, his businesses, one diversion he still found was to give cars away. He didn't actually give away all that many, three that I know of, but doing so pleased him more than almost anything else: I think he liked the sheer absurdity of the gesture as much as its grandiosity. He gave one car to the cleaning woman who worked for them—she was the one who'd re-placed the woman whose husband had sued him—then another to one of his brothers, his own Cadillac, nearly new, which had been stolen from the parking lot at his office and which, though it was recovered the same day, he never was comfortable with afterwards: he must have felt befouled by the fact that a thief, probably black, had been driving the car; and another, the first, the one that gave him the most pleasure, was the one I've already mentioned, which he gave to the rabbi of his syna-gogue. I don't know how he and the rabbi, who was much younger than he was, had become so friendly; I think they'd spent some time fund-raising together, but my father liked the rabbi, who in turn was clearly in awe of my father. At my father's funeral service the rabbi spoke of him as a "giant of a man," but made a rather dim gaffe in telling how he'd once remarked to my father how attractive he must be to women, how many offers he must have had, and my father had replied that when he'd declined the favors of the women who tried to seduce him, he'd always tried to flatter them. (The year before he died, when the tumors in his brain were already beginning to affect him, though none of us realized it yet, he took it into his mind at a New Year's Eve party that my mother was flirting, or had even been making love, with another man, and he attacked her for it. The thought was foolish, that wasn't at all my mother's tendency, but in telling me about it, she said: "He's had enough women himself . . ." thereby disclosing ancient secrets of which I'd had inklings but had never until then had confirmed.) The rabbi, anyway, a pleasant enough man, then went on in his eulogy to tell how one day when he'd picked my father up in his car, a beat-up old compact, my father had said, " 'This is no car for a rabbi to be driving,' and the next morning," the rabbi reverently told us, "there was a new Oldsmobile in front of my house."

*We were kids together, my father and I. Natu-*
*rally, even when I was very young, he was in-*
*volved most of the time in serious matters—just*
*trying to keep food on the table took much of his*
*energy and attention—but in those first years,*
*when he came home at the end of the day and*
*we'd had dinner, he'd give himself to me in a*
*way he never did again, to me or perhaps to*
*anyone else. We'd listen to the radio together, or*
*he'd read the comics to me or one of my books,*
*and sometimes we'd play together on the floor in*
*the living room. One game I loved was when*
*he'd crouch on his hands and knees and let me*
*crawl on him, over him, under him, between his*
*arms and legs. I'd try to bend his rigid arms so*
*that he'd fall; I'd tug, I'd put my whole weight*
*against one arm, or both; I'd push against them*
*like Samson against the columns of the temple,*
*but I never could budge him. Then suddenly*
*he'd let himself collapse, the whole mass of him*
*falling onto me; I'd be terrified he might crush*
*me, but his weight would be suspended hugely*
*just above me: I'd be transported with joy.*

*Or he would pretend to attack me; he'd*
*assume the stance of a wrestler; his arms spread*
*in half-circles like an enormous spider, he'd gri-*
*mace menacingly, the tendons would stand out*

in his neck, the muscles swell in his shoulders, his mouth would become an open arc of aggression; he'd be someone else, someone appalling and ominous. In fear and awe I'd behold him: I couldn't bring myself to go near him when he was like that; though I knew he was making believe, I could only stand back, saying, "No, stop," or something like it, something like, "That's enough, please, be yourself again." Or I'd just wait in openmouthed terror until he'd laugh, and snatch me up to kiss me.

He often read to me at bedtime, too, at first because he just liked to, then later when he was already preoccupied with business, because I was often afflicted with excruciating attacks of poison ivy, would have a difficult time falling asleep, and his voice, or perhaps just his attention, helped me to drift off. He read poetry from an old anthology—I liked "Hiawatha" best, and "The Highwayman"—and he told me tales from the Greek myths, about Hercules especially, and Theseus, the great masculine heroes, but there also was immortally lovely Helen, faithful Penelope, Pandora loosing the evils from her casket, and Medusa, whose glance turned you to stone. He went through some of the Arthurian legends, then made up series of stories for me, one about a wild dog, variations I suppose on The Call of the Wild, and another about an Eskimo who hunted Kodiak bears, the largest, most ferocious mammals on earth.

Before he died, when he was in the hospital for his biopsy and couldn't sleep—he was convinced he hadn't slept for weeks—I thought I'd return that old favor by reading poems to him. Besides, it was hard to do nothing but sit there while he lay for hours with his eyes closed, breathing loudly, with pauses between each inhalation so long that they'd make me think, with relief, wanting his suffering be over, that he'd died, then having him open his eyes again to look grimly at me as though to tell me what I already knew: that he'd hoped the same thing. I felt shy about reading my own poems, so I brought the Iliad and an anthology; the Iliad as a way of recalling and acknowledging the myths he'd told me which became so much a part of my consciousness, and the anthology just in case, which proved to be prescient because when I began to read to him from Homer, I could tell after a few minutes that he wasn't responding, so I suggested that perhaps I should try something else. Good, he said, I hated it back then and I still hate it. How could you have, I thought, when you told me stories that were so much the same? But I didn't say anything; I was only grateful that even if he had hated the myths he'd absorbed enough of them to pass on to me.

The poems he liked best that day were mostly simple lyrics. He'd doze off after I'd read for a few minutes, but as soon as I'd stop he'd jerk awake and ask me to keep reading. We went on for an hour or so, then once when I paused he stayed asleep, as I must have during those long evenings of my childhood, so now I could go out into the corridor and press my forehead against the cool tiles on the wall, and close my eyes, too, and believe I might be resting.

I've wondered what my mother might
have felt during those early years when my
father and I were so close, so much like
best friends; might she have been jealous of
the way we played together? Although all
her life, when she was relaxed and in a
good mood she could be delightful to be
with, she didn't have the capacity for aban-
don, even then, for letting herself be a
child again the way my father could. I
don't mean this to be derogatory, but she
may simply have been too much of a child
herself to dare to act like one. She was always a little childlike in other ways, too;
she was completely and unquestioningly
self-centered, and when she was con-
fronted with adult tasks, like dealing with
someone's suffering, even, as unlikely as it
seemed, her own, she refused to acknowledge the pain completely, but took it
rather as a distraction from the potential
pleasures of whatever hour she was passing
through. When my father was undergoing
his illnesses, his absentmindedness, his depressions, she somehow managed never
quite to submit to them: although she
sympathized with him, wished he were

better, was, you could tell, a little offended without ever saying so by his not being better, she still never manifested what was happening as something that really possessed her; she always kept back that corner of her feelings that might have made her suffer too much. During her own last illness she behaved for the most part the same way toward herself: unless she was flat out in a hospital bed, stunned by chemotherapy, her thoughts would always be turned toward whatever new, agreeable pastime might offer itself as soon as she felt better. The life of pleasure she had chosen was rigorous, it demanded sacrifices, she had to fight always, every day, against anything that might undermine it.

I don't mean to make all of this sound like a fault: it seems as good a way to deal with life's shocks as any other. Though I know I sometimes felt disapproval of the way she acted, and probably asked myself whether there was anything in her vision of life that might have been spiritually redemptive, might have had some meaning beyond itself, and doubted it, it would still surely have been unthinkable to say to her, or to say even to her memory anything like: Stop, you're misusing yourself, yourself and your life, you're missing out on so much possibility. I know if I said something like that even now, I'd only be speaking to myself, to the solemnly self-important person I decided at some point I should be.

There was something touching and even perhaps inspiring about the sheer ferocity of my mother's need to care for her desires; there was even something that could be called virtuous about the way she responded to existence in such a resolutely focused way, how she absolutely refused to take into account any quibbling and fretting about who we are, we human beings, and what we're supposed to be doing.

*What am I doing? I'm making the most of my time on earth in the fullest way I can. This is a conclusion I've arrived at according to all the evidence that has ever been offered to me about existence and its meaning. Furthermore, I can and will suffer for you, in the way I have of suffering; I can feel the utmost sympathy for your pain. But only for the time such suffering demands, and only because the delicate equilibriums I require might be menaced. And I need no understanding from you, no tolerance: this is who I am, you can share it with me with pleasure, or reject me in the service of some specious moral ideal, but you should know you'd be rejecting yourself with me.*

The neighborhood in the city where I live much of the year has several recent immigrant communities in it; all manner of languages, skin colors, styles of living: it makes for a rich atmosphere. Sometimes in a department store or a market I'll see two women together, African, in brilliant voluminous robes and headdresses, or Chinese or Pakistani or Moroccan, who you can tell arrived not long ago in their new country; they don't know the public conventions of being here yet, they stroll through the aisles more slowly than anyone else, take up too much room, talk too loudly or gesture too broadly: they're just a little off.

At first I feel some embarrassment for them, then it comes to me that they're really my mother and my aunt, out shopping after their husbands have started making enough money so that going to the store is a pleasure rather than a challenge and a slight. And they're having such a good time together that they don't care who's watching and possibly judging them. This is too delightful to bother with such trivialities; it's too splendid to be able to saunter here knowing that if you want to buy something—anything—you can: if you like, you can even buy two. So you stop at the watch counter, and you stop to stroke *the leather on a handbag, and you're gabbing all the while to each other, exhilarated by the splendor of it, and with how well it fits you, as though your life had known all along this was to be, to be yours, yet still, if you're my mother, you never mention your good fortune aloud, never for a single instant dare utter how astounding your luck has been: who knows what curse speaking that way might bring upon you?*

Very early on I intuited that my mother's dedication to pleasure was more than simple hedonism, that it was grounded in various systems of anxiety. I realized that to one degree or another she was always afraid, except when her pursuit of pleasure was perfectly focused, her perception of herself in her happiness without flaw, when she felt in short that everything in her world was as it should be, or as much as it could be; then her apprehensions might leave her.

I don't mean to say she was actively haunted by her fears; rather, they were so much a part of her character that she didn't even have to remark them; they were immediately translated into a need to arrange reality so that she wouldn't have to remark them, wouldn't be coerced no matter what into remarking them. On the surface her anxiety was only an edge, it touched just a little into her smile, into the way she'd nervously glance out into the world around her to be certain nothing was out of order, that nothing might be moving toward her with the least potential for evoking the dread she believed always awaited her.

When her fears became more insistent, there wasn't that much of a change: her smile would oval a little, her glance become for the tiniest blink a bit sidelong, not with wistfulness, but wary alertness.

I don't know how that tremulous vigilance had arisen within her. I used to think it was because before she was five she'd lost one younger sister to diphtheria and another who was run over by a car in front of their house, then just at the end of her adolescence her father was killed when his pickup truck skidded on ice into a train. Now it seems to me that though those deaths chagrined her deeply, they weren't enough to explain the sheer doggedness of her uneasiness; if they were perhaps why her anxiety had taken on the force it had, the susceptibility to so much fear had to have already been there within her. I'll say again, though: there wasn't usually any great drama or ado about her anxiety, it was just a fact we all learned to accept. Only at the end of her life, when my father wasn't around to allay her worries, did she sometimes become exasperating; fretting before she'd get into her car about whether she had the proper change laid out on the dashboard for the toll booth, checking three times when she was going on a trip to see whether she'd packed her makeup or a certain dress, or changing her mind ten times about what movie to go to. When we'd spend a night with her at her apartment, I'd sometimes watch her when she came out of her bedroom in the morning; still in her bathrobe she'd look around as though she was actually *seeking* something to fret about. Like the blinded Cyclops mumbling around in his cave having scented something, she'd shuffle into the living room, then into the kitchen, attentive to everything, wanting to make certain everything was in the place it had to be for her to make her breakfast. She'd look genuinely distressed as she set up her coffee maker, assuming it wasn't going to work properly, and when she peered into the refrigerator, she looked as if she was convinced it would be incapable of yielding what she might need from it; then she'd open her apartment door to fetch her newspaper, certain it couldn't possibly be there . . .

There are enough things that happen, Lord knows, to put anyone on edge about chance, and loss, and mortality. My poor mother: I had enough close calls myself to have kept her tingling with angst. One summer during the war we spent a few days at a rather primitive vacation resort in the mountains. After lunch, some other children and I had finished eating and left our tables to wander down to the little river where we used to wade. Though none of us could swim, our parents let us go, assuming we'd play next to the water as we always did. There was a derelict rowboat beached a little way downstream; dried out and decrepit, with gaping fissures in its bottom, it had no oars and only a wisp of rope tied to a ring on its prow. I tried to convince the other kids that we should take a ride in it, and when they didn't want to I managed to haul the boat to the water by myself, and push it in. Then I hopped on, and the current began to take me out toward the deep channel in the middle of the river. The water quickly rose through the hull, reached the gunwales, and the boat started to sink. I was already up to my knees in water, but I decided that when I reached the bottom of the river, I'd just get out and walk along the riverbed back to shore. The boat was almost completely under, I was waiting *for it to sink all the way so I could go over the side when I saw my father racing full tilt down the bank into the water—he was fully dressed and the incongruity of that caused the great splash he made to seem even more spectacular. I was already up to my neck when he lifted me out of the boat and waded back to shore, his clothes pouring.*

*Another time, when I was seventeen, I was working weekends as an apprentice carpenter on one of the housing projects going up then all over the state. I'd been sent to bring some two-by-fours to the house I'd been assigned to, and as I was walking along the dirt service road to fetch them, a truck backed into and then partly over me. I was struck in the side of the head, then shoved along in the dirt for a few yards, hanging on to the bumper to keep from going under the wheels. I didn't lose consciousness, but I'd been hit hard; I was bleeding badly, mostly from my ear, which had been cut nearly in half, and from abrasions down one side of my body.*

*A friend drove me to a hospital where my cuts were washed off, a doctor sewed up my ear, and I was taken to a room where I immediately fell asleep. My friend called my parents—we were an hour's drive from home—and I woke to find my father shaking my shoulder. How are you? he asked. I answered that I was all right, and he said, Well, let's get going. I told him I didn't think they wanted me to leave yet—I was in a lot of pain and still blurry. He went out to the nurses' station, I fell asleep again and when I woke it was the next morning and my mother and father and someone else were in my room. My mother looked stricken, her face drained, her eyes hollow, and she kept glancing at me with a frightening expression I'd never seen before.*

*The person with my parents was a neurologist; he examined me, sticking my toes with pins and touching a thread to my eyeball, announcing finally that I was fine. I found out later that when my father had come home from seeing me the day before, my mother had insisted they call the hospital to get an official report of my condition. Whoever took their call mixed me up with another patient who had had his ear cut in half, too, but who'd been thrown out of a convertible in a violent collision, and badly injured. My parents had been told that they might want to bring their own neurologist to examine me, that I had only a small chance of coming out of the hospital alive and intact.*

*The oddest thing about both those little dramas is that neither my father nor my mother ever spoke of them again. Why did what seemed like natural material for family legends not become them? Surely having your child come that close to death isn't something easily forgotten; though nothing was said, my almost drowning and that night after my accident when my mother believed I might die or be crippled had to have been lurking somewhere in the family's soul. When I became an adult, then a parent myself, I could appreciate the dread there had to have been in it, how, with the drowning, my father afterwards must have thought of having to go back to where we lived without me, his violent desolation and guilt. And my mother: given all her fears about the world, perhaps the notion of losing yet one more person she loved was literally unthinkable; she may very well never have brought it up to herself again, and perhaps she wanted me to forget what happened, too, forget what she would have imagined was my absolute terror in that boat, although in truth I was too naïve to be afraid: I really had believed I'd just walk along the bottom of the river to save myself. And the dread she must have assumed I felt when I lay under that truck in the dirt, scraped raw, bleeding, simply hadn't taken me: I remember even as I was still on the ground I started doing algebraic equations in my mind to make sure my brain hadn't been injured, and as soon as I realized it wasn't, everything else was anticlimax.*

There were two apparently contradictory outcomes of my mother's pervasive fears: the first was that over the course of her life she developed a comprehensive system of regret, a partly domesticated and usually trivial but always efficient mechanism of remorse and contrition. The second, always more surprising to me, was that she was never bored. I'm not certain how her regret grew from her anxiety; maybe it was just a twist of conjugation. Instead of "I might be disappointed or damaged if a certain thing were to happen," there'd be, "I should have done something so that I wouldn't even have had to think of being disappointed or damaged . . ." The conditions of her regret were wildly variable, but never very mysterious. "I should have bought the blue instead of the green dress, I should have taken route 3, I should have stopped smoking when my sister did, then I wouldn't have cancer, I should have made my oncologist's appointment on Thursday instead of Friday."

And usually the regret attacked her not because she actually thought she might have made the wrong choice, but because she worried that she hadn't made the choice that would have been *better*. So her regret was always potentially in force in any matter that entailed the necessity for a decision, and the upshot of her uncertainty was that she often had the sense that she hadn't really made a decision at all, about anything. Choices would be made, but circumstances would always have pushed her too quickly for a reflection full enough so that she could be sure the single undeniable, unquestionable, perfect choice had been revealed, with no trace of contaminating doubt. But such indisputability was rarely vouchsafed to her; a blur of hesitancy always remained to obscure the correctness of her cogitations. The gray of the new bathroom tile was perhaps not a deep enough gray. The car she had just bought possibly wasn't the best make of car to buy just now. Even if you told her it was the most beautiful bathroom, the most impressive car, you'd ever seen, you knew you might make her feel better, but only by keeping her from feeling worse.

How possibly could she be bored then, when she had so much to brood about, so much to ponder? The way certain spirits will meditate on the moral mechanisms of cultures, on metaphysical dilemmas, she would attach herself with an almost ascetic intensity to the advantages or frustrations that awaited her, glinting in the obscurities of future and past. From morning to night, from what to eat for breakfast to which late-night talk show to watch, the world constantly demanded mental exertion. I don't think I ever saw her with nothing to do with her mind; her consciousness leapt with wonderful dexterity from the lurking menaces that might beset her, to the complicated knots of doubt that might make her rue taking both metaphorical and literal wrong roads.

She rarely had to enact many of her anxieties, though, because everyone who knew her knew she had to be protected, cheered, reaffirmed. When my father was alive, he took it for granted that no matter what they were doing he'd have to reassure her that everything was going along as it should be. And I, even still at the age when she'd dampen a comb to scrape through my hair, would catch her air of concern and worry lest my cowlick resist and upset her. Or when, beset by the trivial acne of my teens, I'd let her squeeze out my pimples as the dermatologist had taught her, she'd do it with such evident disquiet and such intense concentration that if my father happened to see us he'd explode at us both, making me feel infantile and ashamed, but distracting her only a moment from what she knew was an unquestionably virtuous task, then she'd go back with her little chrome tool to the next blackhead.

Everyone who knew her took her worries into account. Her friends made sure in the most subtle ways that she'd have the right chair at the right table in a restaurant or at a party. The waiters at her golf club would go out of their way when she came for lunch to make certain she saw that her arrival was a special event; she'd be taken to her favorite corner of the room, and be brought coffee without having to ask for it (although she'd often find it not quite hot enough, or too strong or too weak).

Even when she was undergoing chemotherapy for her cancer, when I went there with her for lunch one day, a woman was at the next table who was suffering from advanced breast cancer and who comforted my mother with such solicitude that you'd have thought the sole purpose of her own illness was to be able to reassure my mother that she was having the proper treatment, the expected symptoms, and that everything would be all right, she'd be well in no time. Though in no time, no time at all, both women would be dead.

Twice, or twice that I know of, my mother's anxiety was displaced by anger, so much so that she completely lost control. Both times were with me. I once heard her shouting at my father: I woke up to hear her hurling across the room the money box they used to keep in their closet: what I gathered in my half-sleep was that my father had loaned their last thousand dollars to one of his customers, who'd proceeded to skip town. I don't know why my mother was quite so angry, she must have been counting on the money to buy something, but she never allowed herself to express real fury with my father, and she didn't quite that time either. Yet, once when I was sixteen, and once again a few years later when I was almost an adult: rage, ferocity, a storm of nearly hysterical wrath.

The first time, I'd been sick, perhaps still wasn't completely well. Nothing serious, I don't even remember, maybe a flu of some sort. I'd come down in the morning and unfolded the sleeping couch in the den and was watching stupid daytime television, and smoking; I smoked already, though not very much. My mother was in the kitchen—the rest of the family was gone for the day—came in to ask me if I wanted anything, and saw I had a cigarette in my hand.

*She knew I smoked, so did she, everyone did in those days, but she said something about it being better not to smoke when I was sick. She looked the way she always did in the morning, a little dour, as though she was resentful at having had to wake up.*

*She went out of the room, and came back a few minutes later with the cord from an electrical appliance in her hand. I thought she was looking for the iron or the vacuum cleaner, but she suddenly began screaming at me, Get up! Get up! and began to lash me with the cord. She hit me a few times, still screaming something, by then I couldn't tell what. I was frightened and appalled, not by pain, though the plug at the end of the cord did bite into my legs, but by her face—it was distorted with fury; she seemed literally beside herself. I think now: Gorgon, Medusa, a tragic mask, and there was that about it, her still uncombed hair wildly framing her face, her mouth torn open by the force of her shrieks, her voice a howl of brute rancor. I began to shout back at her, Mom! Mom! It was as though she was unconscious and I was trying to call her back to herself, and I suppose she was unconscious, in a trance of anger, lost to herself, oblivious to what she was doing, and why she was doing it.*

*She stopped finally; I wasn't crying, or there weren't any tears, though there might as well have been, I'd certainly felt enough terror at how my world had all at once seemed to alter, as though some new mode of sense had been opened in me that I didn't want to have to know about. We stared at each other, then she went upstairs, and soon came down and went out. All that time I just lay where I was on the couch; I don't know what I was thinking, this was before I ever realized I was thinking. I imagine she'd have driven away in her car and come back later on in the afternoon. I know that when we saw each other again at dinner, neither of us said anything about what happened; we must have both still been stunned, and I can't remember when her eyes and mine finally could meet again. In her last years, when sometimes she'd be taken by nostalgia and would talk about the days when I was young, she never brought up that morning, and neither did I. Perhaps we were both still awed by what had happened to her, to us. And when she lashed out at me nearly the same way again, I never put the two experiences together; they must have had similar causes, though I never dared even hypothesize what they were.*

As my mother came to feel more financially secure, after all of us had gone to college and left home and she and my father had moved to a more luxurious house and she drove expensive cars, there were longer and longer periods when her disquietude was allayed, her anxieties stilled, when she appeared to be enjoying life much more than she had before. On the other hand, my father as the years passed seemed much of the time to be bored almost beyond endurance. It felt as if the affliction of his ennui, his submersion in its grinding tedium had become the normal state of his consciousness, the matrix from which all his other thoughts and feelings arose. When he was with friends, playing golf or cards at his club, he'd seem as content as anyone else, smiling and joking; but without active distractions, that other mood would take him, he'd become somber, his gaze would be sluggish, easily fixed on nothing, and you were always conscious that wherever his indifference and apathy came from, their intensity determined how you would have to deal with him: sometimes speaking to him was like disturbing someone in a profound sleep.

There was a time when I thought his bleak moods had to do with me, that it was I who depressed him, that his dark emotions came from something between us. I realize now that although there were enough tensions between us, Lord knows, in this case I was wrong. The unresponsiveness, the malaise, the disinterest, were all his: they had become the condition which all else in his world had to break through before he could regain sufficient enthusiasm to bring him back into an active relation with anyone or anything else.

I used to think that his apathy and low spirits might have had origins in his partial retirement, that there wasn't enough of a challenge to keep him involved in his day-to-day life. He still ran his businesses in those days, still kept watch on them and spoke often to his managers, but there seemed to be little that gave him real satisfaction. He'd tried several times in the past to go beyond his basic sales business by manufacturing office machines himself, but both times it had ended in a disaster from which he was only rescued by selling out to a larger company. By now he must have known he didn't have the ardor or the stamina for the next stage of wealth that kind of expansion might have brought him, but if he regretted it, he never said so, and there'd certainly been enough successes so that he had everything he needed and wanted. In a way he'd domesticated his businesses; all the actual commercial activity happened in other states; near home he had a small office with a few women who did invoicing and billing: he really didn't even have to go there, and when he was in Florida with my mother, he took care of everything on the phone. Even the women he had working for him then weren't at all interesting. When I was young and he still had his office downtown, he had two secretaries neither of whom was particularly pretty but who had remarkable figures; both were busty and slim-waisted, one tall, the other nicely compact, the tall one a brunette, the shorter a blonde. I used to wonder whether he had affairs with them; I certainly mooned about them myself, and once, when he and I were walking out of the office, the blonde, whose desk we had to pass, scribbled something on a sheet of paper and held it up for him to read, and as I came by and tried to glance at it, too, she crumpled it up so I couldn't. A love note? The woman was pregnant at the time; I sometimes wondered if it might have been my father's child she was having, but I never heard anything more about her, so it seems unlikely.

Before those last years, when he was still working so many hours every day, I remember my father saying that he'd like to have a business where the only thing he had to deal with was money, no salesmen, printers, collators, repairmen, truck drivers, secretaries, whatever, but now that he had it, it seemed it didn't take up enough of his energies, and when he went into his darkest depression, after learning that he had prostate cancer, all his free time gave him the chance to brood more than I'd have ever thought he would have on his illness, and perhaps on his disintegrating sense of himself.

Considering the shape of his life, though, how much of himself he gave to his work, how he'd labored for so many years, it's also likely that it wasn't only boredom that beset him at the end, but more of a pervasive weariness, a physical and spiritual exhaustion that

became so much a part of his character that he was sat-
urated in it, dyed by it, tanned, like leather. And maybe
life can just become insufferably tedious: knowing that
you're going to go on as you always have, with the same
days, the same nights, whether you're working your
brains out or have retired into what's supposedly com-
pensation for all your effort but which really makes you
feel you're all but dissolving in your own sense of repet-
itiveness. The last thing my father would have wanted
from me was my pity, but I can't imagine what else to
feel for what he was going through then; it was as
though the exhaustions of all the long working days of
his life had accumulated in him, and that even his successes were taking a perverse vengeance on him.

*My mother hated the places where we lived during those hard early years. In the first flat I can remember with any accuracy, she and my father didn't even have a room of their own; they slept in the living room. We had the lower right corner of a dismal building with three other apartments in it. There was never any direct sunlight in the place, except in the small bedroom at the end of the apartment which was mine at first and which I shared with my brother after he was born. Its window looked out into the backyard, a strip of concrete in front of a garage; I often climbed out the window, sometimes to escape into the dusk to play with the other children on the block when my parents thought I was in bed, sometimes just because it was the quickest way out.*

*Next door to our house there was a collapsed structure people in the neighborhood called "the foundation." The cellar of a building that must have been planned to be the same as ours, it was filled with debris: broken bricks, chunks of concrete and cinder block and asphalt; it looked like an ocean of stone. I spent hours teaching myself to walk then to run from one end of it to the other, memorizing the position of each surface, its angle and its steadiness, until I could race across it at full speed. I was always* running in those days; I'd already learned from my father how fast and hard you were supposed to go through your life, and from my mother how urgent it was not to fall behind.

I even ran in my dreams: our apartment's back door gave out onto a long, dim hallway with three or four steps up to our door, which was the scene of a nightmare I kept having: I'd be running down the hall trying to get away from someone or something, I'd just reach the steps up to our door, and then, though I was still trying to run, I'd no longer be moving, and whoever or whatever wanted to capture me would be terrifyingly upon me; I'd wake screaming. My mother used to tell me that I often woke crying out in the night.

One evening the building was hit by lightning. My mother and I were alone in the apartment, I was in the kitchen by myself when there was the shattering concussion of a lightning bolt, which we found the next morning had struck the roof and torn off the corner of an eave. When the lightning hit, my mother came running to me and I to her and we fell into each other's arms, both terrified. Another evening, I was in the little pantry in our kitchen when a window behind me somehow slammed shut by itself. I wasn't really startled all that much but I screamed; I didn't know why, maybe I wanted my mother to rush to hold me again, but when she threw open the door of the pantry and realized nothing had happened, she was furious and slapped me, hard; that was the first time I felt the full force of her fears.

But her anxieties were always a part of our lives. When my father bought me a penknife, she made him dull the blade. He scraped it back and forth on a block of wood, telling me at the same time that a dull knife made worse cuts than a sharp one. Was that true? Why was he dulling it, then? Was he already telling me something about my mother?

Sometimes my father would mock her worries. When I

started to play football, she wanted me to stop, and my father asked her sarcastically whether she wanted me to stay home and knit. I liked how that joined my father and me in a masculine world which excluded my mother. My father had already long seemed heroic to me, and that perception was often reinforced. Once an old, squarish black Model T Ford rolled over at a corner down the street from where we lived, and my father and some other men turned it back on its wheels. I can still picture how my father looked with the others; it was my first realization that he was taller than everyone else. My memory holds him there, the car half-righted, he leaning at an angle counter to it, heaving mightily against it as though he were bringing it upright all by himself.

In those days he would whistle when he walked up the driveway after work, two tones, one rising, one falling. It was the best moment of my day; I'd rush out and throw myself into his arms. Once, though, he was late; it was very dark when the doorbell rang; I ran to answer and was thunderstruck to find my father slumped against the wall in the front hallway. He was violently drunk, though I had no idea that's what was the matter; I thought he was sick. He staggered in without noticing me and fell like a great tree across the bed. My mother ran to the kitchen and came back with a metal basin that she put on the floor next to his head—I didn't know why she did; I was terrified by it—and shouted at me to go to sleep. It was the only time I ever saw him let himself go like that; from then on, no matter how much he drank, he never seemed to do more than relax a little, become more companionable; and, during the bad times, less actively antagonistic.

*You sell yourself, not what you're selling:* to all the salesmen who ever worked for him, including, for one dreadful, interminable summer, me, my father promulgated that bit of advice. "The products are pretty much the same," he'd say. "Get close to the buyers, get them to like you and trust you, and they'll buy anything you want them to." Over the years, I heard from different sources that he was considered one of the best salesmen in the country, and he was quite aware of it. One evening when I was teaching at a college in another state and he and my mother came to visit us, they spoke at length about their lives. I don't know what brought about so much intimate revelation from them; it had never happened before and never would again. Maybe it was my having a position at what they considered a prestigious place, maybe we'd drunk more wine than usual, but they began to tell us how things had been for them when they were young and poor, which was a story I already knew, but then they began to talk, too, about the years when my father first started to do very well, at the end of the war, which I hadn't heard about until then. Before the war, my father had worked for a large corporation, and after those hard years in which he hadn't earned enough to live on, he became a star salesman, meeting and then doubling his quota every year. Then the company took him off commission, probably because he'd started to make too much money. He was indignant, quit, and so was out on his own. He told us a few of the things he'd done; he'd started an answering service, then some other little businesses, until finally he decided to go back into sales, and opened his first office. When the war ended, he said, I had a lot of ways to go; I could have sold real estate if I'd wanted to, or cars, or even airplanes, but I chose carbon paper. Why carbon paper? I asked. Because it was the most competitive business I could think of, he answered. Then why that? Because I knew I was good, he said.

I was taken aback. It was so out of my ken, almost inconceivable in those days for me to think of my own abilities with such brash confidence. But my father told us about his decision with as much simple factuality as he said he felt at the time. *Because I knew I was good.*

Still, his business didn't always go well. There were ups and downs, printing jobs botched, good customers lost; it must have been very wearing. Once, my father was taking my wife and me to the airport and had someone else in the car he was going to drop off too, an executive from a company that manufactured machines my father sold. The person was talking to me about what an amazing salesman my father was, how he'd made the biggest sale in the history of the business, four hundred machines at one time, to an insurance company. The man didn't know, as I did, that the sale wasn't a sale, and that the whole affair was a disaster. My father had realized some time before that the largest profit was made not on the machines he sold—he'd long ago expanded his operations from carbon paper to form-printing to business machines—though selling them required the greatest effort and expense. The real money was in the supplies customers had to buy to use them; he decided he might as well give the machines away, so he did. He offered the insurance company the four hundred machines for nothing, on condition that they'd contract to buy all their supplies from him, and they took him up on it. I think, in truth, it was like the cars he gave away: he was pleased by the effect the deal would have as much as by the potential profit.

What happened, though, was that there was a fire in a branch office of the insurance company, and it turned out that though it hadn't been a factor, one of the materials the machines used was flammable, which violated a fire ordinance, and the machines were returned. So my father, who'd borrowed a lot of money to pay for the machines, had, as they say in that world, to eat them. All the time this fool was talking about my father's great salesmanship, my father was wondering how to get rid of four hundred used machines, and how to pay off the bank he'd borrowed from to buy them, but you'd never have known any of that. He laughed with the other man, chatted with us; it was, really, as though he *had* eaten his disappointment and his discouragement: he was as cool and composed as someone actually relishing his profit.

I had to admire him that day, although my admiration certainly was nothing new. In childhood, I'd esteemed him with an almost primitive fervor. I would tell my friends much too often what a great athlete he'd been, how physically powerful he was, how successful. My veneration was absolute and unquestioning, at least during those years before . . . before what? Before he began to act more like a boss than a father, before the conflict began between us which neither of us would ever really understand? Before whatever it was, he glowed for me, he was fire and air.

*You sell yourself.* There are almost too many Faustian overtones in that phrase. To give yourself to the devils of commerce: what would the price you'd have to pay finally be? When I saw my father's imperturbability with that machine-company person, when I realized how he could control himself so completely so as not to lose face, I admired him again, but I had an inkling then of what it really costs to sell yourself, how you can end up toughened like scar tissue, and weary, so weary, of everyone you have to deal with, and, possibly, of yourself as well.

*Toughened enough so rage and contempt come to be your natural state of relation with your family, your children, and even your wife? Weary enough so that you have to hoard your moral energy, so the interchange of emotion between you and those you love becomes too costly an outlay for you, and you close down, seal yourself up, your willfulness becomes remorselessness, and your release of feelings out of that harsh arena becomes layered in so much complication that when there is an exchange it feels not like an offering, but an affront; a challenge rather than a communion?*

*"What's the matter?" my father more than once said to me after he'd hurt me. He said it not as a way to conciliate, not as way to allow me to tell him what I felt, not as he had when I was a child and he'd punished me and was ready to comfort me. He said "What's the matter?" with the same curt acrimony with which he'd aggressed me. What he was telling me was that I had the right to attack in turn, but that unless I did so with an equivalent vehemence, I'd prove myself weak, cowardly, unmanly. He was offering a wager, a dare: how much do your precious feelings mean to you, he was saying; do they mean as much as your entire relation with*

*me? As the past and future of your being in the world with me? And because his cruelty seemed to erupt from the very deepest part of him, I knew I'd have to respond from an equivalent place in myself, I'd have to put everything I valued of myself into my counterattack.*

*What kept me from that? I think now that it might have been the irrevocability with which the conflict was defined. If I did attack in my turn, if I had found the acrimony in myself to answer cruelty with cruelty, I knew there could be no going back, because even if I hadn't heard yet of his resolution never again to apologize, I had to have intuited it, and I knew that the only response to my attack that would have satisfied me would have been for him to say he was sorry, and if that wasn't forthcoming, there'd no longer be a relationship at all.*

*My father and I during our worst times came close to that. There were moments when I did challenge his coldness, his harshness, his severity, but never with the unremittingness I needed in order to have real satisfaction. That I didn't, I think, was because, simply, I needed him, not for material matters, but in a much more elemental way; I needed to have him to refer to, to have my life refer to: I needed his acknowledgment of me, even if it often turned out to be disapproving, even if it was never articulated at all. Because I had loved him so long, and perhaps feared him and sometimes loathed and raged at him, I couldn't imagine not having him there in an active way in my life: as someone I'd loved in the past, he wouldn't do.*

*I'm sure he felt something like this, too, some need, some irrevocable connection to me. I wasn't easy; I was contrary, headstrong, and in many ways smarter than he was: I could always come out ahead in discussions with him, about anything that didn't have to do directly with us. We would argue about politics, economics, social problems, foreign affairs, and especially Israel, because I believed in accommodation with the Palestinians, territory for peace, compromise for peace, and he, like many American Jews, found the idea of anything less than a vigilant mistrust of the whole Arab world, the whole non-Jewish world, in fact, to be mortally threatening for Israel, and therefore for all Jews, for himself.*

*We both must have known that such passionate disputes can stand for other things, yet however much we'd affront one another, beat our chests and flash our fangs, we'd both have known, too, that in some absurd way we needed all of it, just as we needed the larger process in which we were embedded, and the culmination of that process toward which perhaps we were moving, and which perhaps we actually accomplished during the last days of his life.*

There was a part of my father that always claimed to crave simplicity, humility, plainness. I remember early on remarking how he would sometimes be taken by a fit of what I suppose was nostalgia and, instead of eating the dinner the rest of us were, he would make himself a plate of rice and milk, and sprinkle some sugar on it, or he'd open a can of tomato herring, slice onions into it, and with a chunk of bread make that his meal; he made it look delicious. In those years he'd often take me with him on Sunday mornings to shop in the delicatessens down in what was left of the old Jewish neighborhood; he knew a lot of people there, and obviously enjoyed being with them, speaking a little Yiddish. The first time I heard him speak it I was astonished; I'd had no idea he knew any, though my grandparents often spoke it. Even when he'd become successful, he'd sometimes tell my mother he didn't want to go out to the restaurant she'd planned on, that she should just make a can of soup for him, which would irritate her no end. Although I always interpreted those odd reversions as relating to something in himself, some longing or dissatisfaction, I could tell my mother took them as a repudiation of the life she'd participated in making with my father. And in truth, the way they lived, the degree of luxury they partook of, were largely her doing: my father would sometimes complain about the amount of money they spent, not because he didn't have it, but because when he was in that mood he would find it intrinsically repugnant to waste so much.

Maybe his nostalgias were partly a slap at my mother, but I think he did have genuine glimpses of a way of life that would have suited him better than the one he had, that in some ways he felt he might really be someone else, someone who would indeed live more simply, with more . . . I'm not sure what: meaning, I suppose. When I visited Jerusalem, I was wandering one afternoon through an ultra-Orthodox neighborhood, not enjoying at all what I took to be such a reactionary and fanatical way of living; I felt no sympathy with the Hasids and their absurd eighteenth-century costumes, the wide-brimmed black hats, black coats and pants—some of the men even wear knickers, with knee-high white stockings, and patent-leather slippers. Yet as I strolled there, I suddenly visualized my father, dressed just as bizarrely as these men were, and I realized that perhaps he really could have been quite happy living like that, in a community with strict, unbending rules and prescribed modes of behavior, in which even one's dress is a pointed affirmation of the presumably sanctified world, inner and outer, to which one is committed. And my father could, actually, be quite puritanical: for a long time he wouldn't tolerate from any of us language he considered obscene (though we'd hear him use the words himself with his friends), and he was furious and wanted to throw my brother and me out of the house when he caught us smoking marijuana at my sister's wedding party.

It's almost impossible to describe the delight my mother took when we moved into our first house. This was before the empty money box, before so many other scratchings and hackings at the surface of my parents' marriage: my father, I'm sure, shared in my mother's pleasure, but she was exultant, triumphant. We moved there after that gloomy apartment with its nightmare hallways, and though in the same neighborhood, it was on a street where there were only other "one-family houses," which was absolutely essential to my mother. The house was small, and, when I think back to it now, decidedly ungainly-looking, but it had an unpretentious, companionable feeling about it, and I enjoyed it especially because although I still had to share a room with my brother, we had a real backyard now where a friend of mine and I put up a backboard and basket, and there was an empty lot next to the house with a great glacial boulder in it that fascinated me and that I liked to sit on.

The whole while my mother was getting the house ready, she was pregnant. After two sons and a scary miscarriage in a thunderstorm on a vacation in the mountains—she told me about it once; an awful night—she dearly *wanted a daughter; my sister was born soon after we moved in, and she, too, in her pink-and-white bedroom, seemed to have arrived as an element of my mother's idea of domestic perfection.*

*We had lived there only a few years, though, when my mother, and then I suppose my father, decided to move to the suburbs, only three or four miles but a class or a class and a half away, or so we were given to think. I went back to that first house a few years ago, driving through what had been the pleasant edge of a city; now there were high public housing buildings nearby, the stores I'd known all had iron shutters over their windows, and, what I found most disturbing, four or five houses had been built on the empty lot beside what had been our house. I realized then that much of my memory of the place had focused on that field of scrubby weeds with its boulder like something in a Zen garden, and much less on the house itself, probably because it was where I first became conscious of how my parents' anger toward one another and their furious silences could fill rooms like the odor of fresh paint my mother so relished.*

A rather formal photograph of my father hung on the wall of the conference room of his main sales office; he'd had it taken himself, perhaps because in the last years of his life he was so seldom there. After his death, with my brother running the business, the photo began to appear on brochures and advertisements; it was meant to embody the long history and presumed reliability of the firm. As the years passed, it must have been reproduced from other reproductions, so that over time my father's features became more and more schematic, until, by the time the business was sold a dozen years after his death, it didn't look like a photograph of him at all but like a blotchy print of some paradigmatically forceful and trustworthy youngish executive. I found the image disturbing the last time I saw it; I wondered whether it would interfere with my father's features in my mind, but it didn't—I can still call his image up whenever I want to, with whatever expression I want him to have.

I usually like to remember him smiling: he had one particular smile that during the years of animosity between us, and then later, when he was in his depressions about being ill, I rarely saw—broad, unrestrained, entirely frank. When he'd smile like that, you'd notice as you wouldn't otherwise that there was a space between his front teeth, a gap that acted as a sort of stress mark, emphasizing his expression.

When he was in an especially expansive mood, for an hour, or an evening, and he'd smile that way, there seemed no qualification to how he'd respond to you, no limit to how ready he was to welcome you into his warmth. Perhaps I've made him sound as though he was always as dour as he was complex, but that wasn't the case; he could be thoroughly charming. Most people found him quite amiable, and with most people he was. He had many friends, all of whom thought highly of him, and there were many people he barely knew, neighbors, merchants, people to whom he'd hardly said more than hello, who spoke fondly of him: when he died, my mother received a number of condolence letters from people she'd never met.

When he was in that benign mood, his pleasure was wonderfully infectious; it was remarkable how he attracted people, how he could make them feel that something uncommon was happening to them when they were in his company. Even his children, even his son; even if you were still scraped raw by whatever abrasion he'd last inflicted on you, you'd feel both relief and an odd sense of fulfillment at being allowed to participate in his good spirits.

When he decided—no one could ever say why he would or wouldn't—to let his kinder nature be revealed, even his physical presence became welcoming.

His ordinarily prodigious and forbidding heft would subtly alter so that his volume now would include you, incorporate and enlarge you. No wonder the rabbi would call him a giant, and no wonder humans are so taken with giants, with how they can induce awe and a sense of shared power in us. No wonder, too, that we're so prone to look for the giant's weakness, so he can be diminished and brought down.

One Sunday—I don't remember how old I was—we went, just he and I, to a park where people came to watch and feed a small herd of deer caged in a paddock. I was wonderfully pleased to be out alone with him, but I could see he was preoccupied, so I left him and wandered farther down along the fence. I was poking my fingers through the wire, trying to get a fawn to lick my fingers, when I heard a man say to someone with him, "They're always dumb when they're that big." I knew they had to be talking about my father; I looked toward him and saw him standing where I'd left him, still in whatever train of thought had captured him, and, indeed, he did look if not stupid then unalert, unaware. His mouth was a little too open, his gaze too fixed. I knew he was surely thinking about business, but I was furious and humiliated by what the man said and I went over to my father and told him I wanted to go home. I didn't really, but I wanted him to stop looking the way he did, and I wanted those men to see the expensive car he drove; I wanted to prove to them that he was hardly stupid, that he was surely richer than they were, and so had to be smarter.

That's what I thought then: I know now that what was most important for me was to expunge from my own consciousness the least potential truth those words might have had: they hinted at such an unthinkable proposition, largeness and dullness, rather than tallness, therefore uniqueness, even possibly, probably, nobility. I'm tall myself, so is my brother, though neither of us is as tall as my father was, and it was always assumed in our family, and for a long time I believed it, that being tall was virtuous in itself, no matter what else you might be or do: it wasn't until I was well into middle age that I realized how preposterous that conceit was.

But I think my father never stopped thinking it. One evening, when he and my brother and I were in a restaurant, and a friend of my father's approached our table, a man of ordinary height, my father whispered, "Get up," and the three of us stood all at the same time, dwarfing the person. Though his friend didn't find the joke all that funny, my father laughed with delight. My father's laughter when he was pleased to be where he was, doing what he was doing, carried with it an extraordinary sense of approbation. If she was there, my mother would visibly come into herself, her smile would brighten and her gladness would be such that even if there were only four or five of us, she would act as though we were having a party; though she might not have a new dress, a new hairdo, new perfume, she'd still be that joyful. Even during the very hardest years with my father, if his benign mood took him, you'd leave their company feeling as though you'd been celebrating something, perhaps just the fine fortune of having all been together. And you'd never think what had been celebrated was my father's not being in his other humor, his other mode of connection, when his darkness or his anger determined the ambiance of your meeting. Even when he was feeling good, though, when he became tired, or if he felt what was going on had lasted too long, there would be a sudden slackening in him that you could sense even in his body: he'd seem to be looking at you from lower in the space he occupied than he had been; that gap in his teeth, the stress mark that italicized his good spirits would be concealed again. All at once, when you said something you meant to be amusing, he'd be looking at you with a somber cynicism, as though he didn't understand not only how you could say something so foolish, but how you could even think of inflicting your foolishness on him. "Let's go," he would say abruptly to my mother if we were out, or, if we were at their house, he'd say to me, "It's late, you better get going." We'd know then that our audience with that agreeable part of him had come to an end, and so, carefully, warily, hardly daring to look back, we'd leave.

Is it disappointment one experiences at such moments, during such an after-climax, or shame or resentment, as though you'd been gulled, as though you'd been had? Either way, disappointment, anger, shame, you'd know that the next time with him might work out well, and you'd be thankful for the possibility that you might be with him again when he was at his best, affectionate, charming, engaging, embracing.

*Once, in a book on the second World War, I came across a photograph from the last days of the Warsaw Ghetto of a group of Jewish men surrounded by a squad of German soldiers. What was going on wasn't clear; the Jews were standing in a driving rain, apparently waiting for something, perhaps a distribution of rations, perhaps work, perhaps the transport to a camp. One of the men was much taller than the others; he wore a battered hat and a worn overcoat much too small for him, and he was gaunt and haggard, his jaw unshaven, his face not so much expressionless as stricken with impassivity, as though it contained nothing, no emotion, no thought, no hope, worth bothering to express anymore. I had never thought of those who'd died in the Holocaust as tall or short, fat or slim, but now, because of the man's height, and perhaps, too, because of the grim blankness of his expression, I found myself seeing my father in him, then to my surprise I saw myself in him, too, so for a horrid instant my father and I fused into that surely perished soul, our shoulders hunched against the smeared, ashy rain; freezing, frightened, already overwhelmed by our hideous extinction.*

At the party celebrating my brother's second marriage, my father announced to my mother early in the evening that he wanted to leave. I couldn't blame him, he knew hardly anyone there, just as I didn't—I left soon after, too—but my mother wanted to stay: for her, a party was a party; she was feeling gay and looked vivacious, and she tried to talk him into staying. My father insisted, though, and she acquiesced, albeit a bit petulantly, and my aunt, my mother's sister, who had to leave, too, because she and her husband had driven to the party with my parents, said to me as they were going, "Your father's not a well man." I didn't know at the time how to take what she meant. Was she saying she was irritated with my father for making her leave; or that he was physically ill, which was no news—he'd had his cancer for a long time by then—or did she mean that he was losing his emotional bearings, which also had been happening for such a long time that it seemed to me to be hardly worth remarking? I couldn't tell.

Not long after that, my family and I went away for some months, and as soon as we came back I called my mother to ask how things were. She answered, "Pretty good," which as I've mentioned could mean anything from a minor problem to a full-blown catastrophe, but since I'd told her we were coming to visit the next day, I didn't press her.

When we arrived she said my father was out in back, which was unusual, I'd never known him to stay in the yard by himself. When I went out, and found him, I was stunned. He was sitting in a lawn chair, a cane across his knees, his back was curved so much he looked almost hunchbacked, he was much thinner than the last time I'd seen him—horribly shrunken—and he was staring bleakly into space. My God, I thought, he looks like an old Jew, a weak, thin, pale old Jew. Such an absurd thought: of course he was an old Jew, but this was more than that. He seemed to have lost so much of himself, his cancer and the waste of his sadness had so diminished him that, trapped in the ruins of his frame, he wasn't so much not himself as no one at all. He seemed to know it, too; he looked at me with a helpless expression I'd never seen before, and I felt heartsick for him.

His physical decline accelerated over the next ten days; it wasn't until he'd definitely understood he was dying, that there was nothing more to be done, that his aphasia would only get worse over whatever time was left him, and he'd resolved to kill himself and finish all that and had found a way to accomplish it, not until then would he inhabit himself again, move back into himself, fill himself so that his ravaged but still formidable container could manifest him once more. As shocking to me as his deterioration had been, that renewal of himself was even more remarkable: it was as though even his body, with all its rotting disease, had been compelled by the sheer power of his will to become in its essence what it had once been, so that the details of its appearance became incidental to the strength of his presence within them. He sat and stood straight again, tall again, and there was also, as I've said, an ease, a surrender, a serenity about almost everything he said and did during that time.

But that was later. Now, that afternoon, when I spoke to him and he lifted his head and saw me, he said, "Hello, don't worry, it's just my screen . . . broken"; then other half-phrases I don't remember that were just as erratic and disturbing. At lunch, he spoke a little more reasonably, but he still used inappropriate, sometimes barely comprehensible words; it was obvious something dire was happening to him: I thought he'd gone out of his mind, that he'd become psychotic, that his depression had taken such hold of him that he'd broken down completely.

When we went home that evening I tracked down an old friend, a psychiatrist who specialized in the treatment of the aged, and made an appointment for my father to see him, but I had to cancel it. During the night, my father, as though his illness had been waiting for me to return to openly declare itself, woke and began to rave to my mother in a way that made it impossible for her to think or say later anything close to "Pretty good": he was trying to explain to her about a jury that had convicted him; that he was going to be executed. Early the next morning she called a doctor, who sent my father to a hospital where they discovered the tumor in his brain, sent him home, where he stayed for a day before being ferried to another hospital, where they burst the vile bubble under his skull, and broke his arm, making certain he wouldn't have enough of himself left to want to go on.

"I'm not supposed to say that, am I?" my father said to me one Thanksgiving Day, as we were watching a football game on television, and, commenting on a spoiled play, he made some appallingly racist remark about a black player, then about black people in general.

"No, you're not," I answered, and, since it was a holiday and I wasn't in a mood to argue, I let the subject drop. I've wondered, though, what happened to change my father's attitude toward race so much; he'd instilled a decidedly liberal outlook in me. I remember when I was an adolescent he and I once saw a black man driving a big new car, the image of which in those days was a cliché supposedly demonstrating black people's lack of reasonable values: it was assumed a black man must be very poor, so a costly car implied a misuse of presumably limited resources. Maybe I said something to that effect, something I'd have picked up from a friend, and my father responded by saying, "You have to understand, Negroes don't have anything else to spend money on: they can't buy decent houses, they can't go to good restaurants, and most of them can't get into college; what else is a Negro who makes some money supposed to do with it?" I felt abashed and took very much to heart not so much that particular observation, though I found it entirely convincing, but rather the dialectic implied in what my father said: it was something he'd have to have considered carefully to have arrived at a point of view which in those days was unusual among the people he knew.

When, so much later, he made that crude, bigoted observation, he must have realized that I'd be the dialectician this time, and that I'd be critical of him. So though he didn't say he was sorry—I knew not to expect that—he did at least qualify his words.

But what had happened to change him so much? Downtown, where he'd had his office for so long, had deteriorated hopelessly by then, the city government was corrupt, as it had been for decades, the city was populated almost entirely by poor blacks and Hispanics, and of course there was the crime that goes along with poverty. In the last years that my father still had his office there, a kind of cage had to be built in the storeroom because so many supplies were being stolen by his own employees. The building that housed his office then wasn't quite an island amid devastation the way many buildings there are now, but it must have been a disagreeable trek for him to drive into the failing city. Later he moved the business out to the suburbs, as many others did, but I think he resented being forced to: he must have felt as though he'd been robbed of the place he knew so well—he'd covered every one of the city's commercial streets on foot during those years he was first setting up his business and was his only sales-man. Still, that didn't account for such a radical change of attitude, and I remember I used to think that it had to have been something personal that would have in-spired him with so much ill-feeling toward blacks. I imagined that perhaps a black man had humiliated him: I pictured a powerful young tough purposefully bump-ing into him, just because he was so big, and then when my father challenged him, the other would have faced him down and mocked him. I didn't have any actual reason for thinking that; though I did hear stories of it happening to some people, it was more likely that I wished my father for once would have to back away from someone, dephysicalize himself, submit.

Maybe, though, he began to distrust and to speak badly of black people after his employee, the ex-chauffeur with whom he'd been such chums, had be-trayed him by taking him to court. But whatever it was that had brought about the change, I was chagrined by it, and I was relieved now that at least he'd responded to my discomfort; his doing so implied if not any renewed social rectitude then at least a sensitivity to my feelings. Later, though, despite the reconciliation we'd effected about almost everything else, he continued to make the same sort of ridiculous racist comments, and every time I'd have to face that his wanting to hurt my feelings was a conscious part of what he said.

Sometimes I've thought that perhaps my father did things like that with me because I'd come to stand for attitudes he'd once admired in himself, but didn't be-lieve in anymore; that might explain some of the appar-ently random animus with which he'd try to offend me.

He knew how intensely I felt about racial inequality, how much of my moral vision was informed by the issue. It occurs to me that he might have resented not so much my political or moral vision as the fact that I had such strong, enduring feelings about the question at all, and about much else he simply didn't trouble himself about anymore. How much of our apparently intimate disagreements might have to do with unspoken conflicts like that; with our realizing that a consciousness with which we're connected is taken up with matters that don't involve us, so we feel abandoned, bereft, and because nothing is worse than indifference, not even pain, to allay our feeling of being slighted or belittled, we pounce and attack.

*When I was as young as ten or eleven, I often wanted to run away from home. There seems to be finally very little I can be sure about how other people have affected me, even in important ways, so I can't say for certain whether I wanted to get away because my parents were fighting so much then, or because my father was so different toward me, or just because I wanted adventure or change. My parents' tensions had quickly become a part of the way we lived; neither they, nor anything else of which I was aware, was particularly troubling me, yet I often felt a terrific restlessness, an irrepressible urge that translated into a need to not be where I was. My favorite books had to do with boys and young men off on their own in the world, on pilgrimages of one sort or another or just wandering wherever their destinies took them. I often hiked or rode my bicycle out of our neighborhood; I felt as though I was looking for something, though I never could tell what. One afternoon after school, alone in the house, I was taken by that wish to flee more intensely than I ever had; I felt a resonant, aching void in my chest which, though the feeling wasn't entirely unpleasant, still seemed to demand that I do something other than go out to find one of my friends or play ball. So I made*

some sandwiches, put them in my knapsack with a sweater, and started walking. I went some miles out into the suburbs; then I got hungry and ate the sandwiches, and that must have made me feel better, or different, or what I was used to, because I went back.

A few years later, on my way to high school one morning, I had the same desolate feeling, and instead of going on I started hitchhiking in the other direction. I kept going from ride to ride, on a general bearing then straight for the house of a friend who lived in the country about fifty miles from us. I didn't really understand why I was going there, maybe I didn't know any place farther from home. It was a brisk, windy day at the end of winter, and when I'd left the suburbs, then the main highways behind, I found myself walking alone on an unpaved road in the country and I suddenly realized I was happier than I'd ever been in my life. That the cold cut through my thin cotton jacket, chilling me, made the feeling even better; that the fallow fields were raw and clean and the trees still had no leaves, the wind rushing through them so loudly that I shouted out once just to hear my voice, made it better, too. The sky was higher than I'd ever seen it, it seemed infinite, pure and transparent, as though the wind had scrubbed it clean, and it felt wonderfully accessible to me. There were no blurrings of surfaces anywhere I looked, there was only the sheen of light radiating from the entire sky rather than from the still low winter sun, so that everything—trees, clouds, the fields stretching into the distance and the sheer unfamiliar sense of my own existence—was vital and vibrant and alive.

My friend was at his house recuperating from a cold when I got there. I spent a few hours keeping him company, but the whole while I felt an unfamiliar loneliness; it must have been the first time I felt nostalgia, not for home, for my *father or mother, but for myself. Perhaps I realized, too, that my just going on, away, into the unknown, had been a real possibility; that if I hadn't had my friend's house to aim for I might well have left home then and there, and perhaps I was feeling regret that I hadn't.*

In the emergency room the resident at first thinks my mother has pneumonia; she had it last winter. "Why would I have it again?" my mother asks: "It's August." Then her own doctor is called and arrives; he chats amiably with her. How can I have pneumonia? she says again. Why don't we see? the doctor replies. He has an X-ray taken of her lungs and calls me over to look at it: there's a massive tumor, her lungs and chest cavity are partially filled with a fluid which when she lies down rises into her bronchia and makes her feel as though she's choking, which in fact she is.

When we were driving back to her apartment earlier that afternoon—it was the day after my daughter's wedding—she fell asleep in the car. My mother adored my daughter; at the wedding party she'd been elated, jubilant, nearly ecstatic, and now, her head to one side, her mouth open, she was very pale, and looked ex-hausted.

When she woke, she said: Why did I do that? Fall asleep? I never do that. You must be tired after the party, I said. Never, she answered, I'm never that tired. I realized she was right, she never did take naps, and I began to worry.

A few hours later she complained she couldn't breathe and I took her to the hospital.

It's a tumor, her doctor tells her now. Why would I have cancer? she says. I haven't smoked for five years. Where would it come from?

Why? She asks why. She wants reasons.

My mother always had to have reasons. For things that went wrong, for things that weren't as they should have been, for things catastrophic or incidental, she would look assiduously, desperately for reasons. Hunting for causes, she naturally was adept at blame. If one of her children was ill, there had to have been a germ, a contagion that should have been controlled. If there was an argument, someone had to have started it, therefore someone had to be wrong; an accident came about because someone made a mistake, therefore, again, someone was at fault, could be held accountable, and thus her craving for reasons would be satisfied, so everyone could feel better, though no one ever did, not even she.

Because, because: there had to be a reason; for a son to choose the wrong profession, to divorce, to . . . it doesn't matter. Along with her general anxiety, there was this constantly being affronted by what was unreasonable to her. Maybe that's what made her so disconsolate about my becoming a poet, and, later, about my refusal to follow her sometimes spoken and always tacit exhortation that I write something, anything, even a dirty book, she actually once said, to make more money. She must have been inwardly incensed that I'd

chosen such an absurd way to live, and, worse, how little I regretted it. That's what troubled her so about my
long hair when I was that age, my beard, the rags I wore
for a while, my travels, my wasting my time not only
with poetry but playing the guitar and piano. Even at
moments when she was clearly pleased to be with me
and was enjoying herself, I knew she would still be trying to figure out why this had happened to her; well
into my adult life she believed there was time for me to
take her doubts more seriously, to reconsider and start
my professional life over. It bothered me, but I knew
she questioned everything else the same way.

So, now that she was very probably mortally ill, it
wasn't surprising that she asked, and kept asking,
"Why?" Not, "When will I die?" or "What can be done
to keep me alive?" Or not until, when she could see
that everything that was being done obviously wasn't
working, she could ask "Why?" about that, too, and try
to find reasons, to accuse. A friend of hers was having a
different chemotherapy: shouldn't she have it? When
the oncologist told her the drug wasn't appropriate for
her cancer, she didn't believe him. Probably the hospital
where she was being treated was inferior to her friend's.
Or her cancer doctor: how could we be sure she'd
found the right one? We couldn't; she probably didn't,
but it wouldn't have mattered.

So, on her cot in the emergency room now, she
says to her doctor: I had a chest X-ray six months ago:
wasn't it there then? We didn't see it, the doctor an-
swers. How can I have it if you didn't see it? The doctor must know her well, he doesn't argue. She looks at
him with indignation. Not with real opprobrium, or

not yet; it's the indignation of the unsatisfied intellect she feels. She really wants to know why. She really wants a reason so . . . so she'll know whom or what to reproach.

"I shouldn't have . . ." I can hear her say, "Why did I . . .?" What she's really saying is, "Why doesn't the world reveal sufficient reasons to me?" Still, she knew there were risks in her obsessive questioning, and she was careful never to go too far. So, when she fell so ill, she had to decide (I can almost hear her deciding) whether to use the word "death" in her interrogations, in her considerations of the circuits of cause and effect, and I know she decided not to, because the word itself had implications too grave, too final. Thus she omitted the word from her reflections, she banished it; like the great poet of death, Rilke, who when he was dying did the same thing, never once during her illness did she use or even hint at the concept. She seemed to pay death no mind whatsoever, but clung resolutely to what was happening to her, even the chemotherapy, the radiation, not to speak of the hours when she was feeling relatively good.

So thoroughly does she suppress the whole notion of death that in the hospital, when I look into her eyes and she looks frankly back at me, I can't sense anything close to it, I can't even imagine it in there with her. If it were in here with me, her eyes say, I might really die. This way, as long as I'm with you, and with others who love me, I'll perhaps be able to go away without dying, I'll simply expire, the way a debt, paid or not paid, expires.

Even when she's dead, in her narrow hospice bed,

my hand moving on her head, so small, I realize, so almost perfectly round, like a child's, there's something about her stillness that seems almost pugnaciously to regret having had to go. Her red hair, dyed these last decades, is gone, only a soft stubble of gray remains, which I stroke, feeling how wonderfully soft yet resistant it is, this last divulgence and declaration of her existence. And yet her expression, still uncomprehending, indignant, proclaims that she doesn't really believe she's dead; she knows, in fact, she hasn't died yet, not really, because no one has explained to her why she should die, nor who is to blame for her dying.

*It used to happen to me just as I was falling asleep, when my consciousness would begin to drift from the world outside to that other awareness within, that I'd hear my mother's voice, calling my name. It wasn't as simple as that, though; the experience was complicated and strange, and though it happened many times, each time I'd have to parse it out again.*

*I'm not sure if it was a dream or not; I had never had the sense that I'd been asleep, I'd just suddenly realize that my mind had become a kind of space: perfectly empty, it had a coarse, grainy, material texture, which, when I tried to examine it more closely, would seem to be inhabited by a deep, resonant vibration, which both defined the space and prevented me from bringing anything else into my consciousness. As I continued listening, I seemed to be taking up a less and less significant part of the volume of my mind, which included somehow even the inner surface of my skull, in which all this was happening.*

*It wasn't an unpleasant feeling, but it was mystifying, and, as I say, I never would remember from one time to the next what was going to happen then, which was that I'd begin to realize that the vibration was a voice, my mother's voice,* saying aloud that single word, my name, in a way that made the sound of it expand, and become more dense, more like an actual physical substance.

Though I could have been afraid, I never was; I'd feel something like the opposite of fear, in fact, as though I was somehow more firmly situated in myself, and in the universe. I could say "universe," because, as a part of all that was happening, there'd be a sense of timelessness, and a conviction that my perception, visual and aural, had rendered any other reality that ordinarily might have come to me. While my mother's voice was there within me, I had no need of anything else: although she was calling me as she had when she wanted me to come to her when I was a child, I knew I didn't have to answer: the way I was contained in my mind, the way my mother's voice rang through it, implied a unity which demanded nothing except my attention.

Next would come a compelling sense of being in proximity not only to her voice but, although I couldn't see her, to my mother herself: her invisible presence was like a concrete thing, elusive, yet infinitely alluring.

Then all of it would stop. I'd come to myself, my ordinary self, the person lying there in my bed. It was such a gratifying experience, though, that when it did stop, when the voice went silent and the space within me lost the materiality it had had, I'd try to make it happen again, but I never could, and there was nothing to do but wait until it came to me again, until I'd hear again so deeply within me the voice of my mother calling my name, calling and calling, as she had when I was a child, and perhaps as she had, silently, within herself then, as she moved further and further into the endlessness of her dying.

The other occasion when my mother lost control of herself, I did, too. It's an evening in my adolescence; I've been watching television in the den with my father, who's waiting for my mother to get ready so they can go out. My mother calls to me to come upstairs, and tells me to do something, I forget what: when I go back down and my father asks me what happened, I say, "She wanted such and such," or, "She said such and such . . ."

And now my mother comes storming downstairs from her bedroom, screaming at me in rage: "How many times have I told you I'm not *she*?" She shouts it at me, then shouts it again, standing so close to me I feel her breath battering my face. Yes, she has told me, yes, fifty, a hundred times, not to refer to her as "she," a pronoun, which I'd always found to be a ridiculous prohibition. But this is different, this time she's irate, incensed: this time I can feel her anger burning into me in a way I never have before, even that other time when she'd beaten me, and now I find I'm furious, too. I begin shouting back at her with so much intensity that, despite her own anger, she falls still.

The words I said to her are gone, but their content was that she was and had always been a failure as a mother, that she was lazy and spoiled, that she'd left me to take care of myself even when I was small, to dress myself and make my own breakfast, had never walked me to school the way other kids' mothers had, that even now she was never at home when I needed her; that all she thought about was herself, the only thing that was important to her was money, and parties and, and . . . I don't remember it all, but as I was accusing her of everything I could think of, I was also sobbing, tears were streaming down my face for the first time since I'd come to puberty and the last for another twenty years or so.

I know my mother was shocked and bewildered by my animosity and heat: she must have known that my little grammatical offense had elicited a response far beyond its seriousness, but I'd answered with a rage I'd never given any indication I felt, and I recited such a compendium of maternal sins—I must have touched on many of the ways she assumed she was a good mother—that she had to have been hurt, which, if I knew it, and I think I did, must in itself have astounded me.

My father sat watching and listening, saying nothing. It only occurs to me now to wonder if my rage might have been directed at him, too; whether these were accusations I didn't dare hurl at him, but wanted to. After all, if I was complaining of neglect, his neglect of me by that time far outstripped my mother's; if the issue was money, surely that was already more his doing than hers: his daily routine and even, already, the way he acted toward me, toward all of us, was more determined than my mother's was by his connection to the world of money.

At last, anyway, I stopped shouting, ran outside, and stayed there until my crying subsided. When I came back in, my father was still in the den, my mother was upstairs again. "Go tell your mother you're sorry," my father said. And I did. I don't know if I was really contrite, or just exhausted, but I went up and apologized. What did she reply? I don't remember. What did I see in her face? She had her make up on by that time; it might have obscured her feelings. Were there repercussions from my outburst? I don't remember that either. Maybe it's not important. Just the memory might be all I need, my shouting at her, my tears, her looking at me in disbelief, and my father impassively beholding us, perhaps relishing—might he really have been?—his feeling of blamelessness.

I don't think I harbored any bitterness or spite toward my mother for all I said that evening nor for her disapproval of so much I did later. Yet I never told my mother about my intriguing experience of hearing her voice in my mind. In the years when I didn't speak of such intimate matters to anyone, there was no question of telling her about it: I was convinced she'd never understand, as she misunderstood so much else about me. Later, might I have kept it from her as a petulant way of getting back at her? I hope not.

Remembering my mother, her voice, her presence, evokes so much solicitude in me now; I wish I had told her about it. Although, perhaps my not having told her had more childish causes; maybe in some way I still felt as I did during those first years, when it wasn't necessary to tell her anything at all about myself, because she already would know. Might that closeness have been something we experienced together in those primal hours when she held me to her in her arms? My eyes closing and closed, my uncertain awareness of myself, my consciousness drifting, her voice leading me down into the sleep that seemed to wait somehow within her as much as within me, perhaps that was all we both needed.

*It's taken so long for me to realize how wounded
my mother really was. I've always known that
her fears controlled much of the way she approached life, but I never really considered where
they came from: I thought they had to do with
the shock of the deaths of her sisters and father,
but those are things that come to any life, they
don't explain the way she became so clenched in
herself all her last decades, so closed to the range
she'd had of emotion and expression.*

*Once, when we were having a family din-
ner, my father told a joke that had to do with
the sexual unresponsiveness of Jewish women.
He thought it was very funny, but my mother
scowled, I thought because she didn't like to
have risqué jokes told around her. Now it occurs
to me that she might have felt slighted by the
joke, or perhaps threatened, and all at once I understand that she wasn't a passionate or very
sensual woman, that it's likely she wasn't very
sexually responsive either, and that perhaps my
father suffered from that and had taken it out on
her in whatever ways those things happen.*

*Maybe that was one constituent of her
pain, I'll really never know, but it's clear there
was something that kept her from ever being entirely at ease; she was always, always a bit on*

*guard, as though she was sheltering some too-sensitive place in her psyche that she didn't want to have touched. Perhaps it wasn't about sex with my father, but I feel it had to have something to do with him, there's no one else who could have inflicted that kind of damage. All the long years of their silent arguments; maybe she'd been ground down by them, and had gradually learned to protect her feelings, to pull herself off to the side of herself, so she didn't have to gaze too carefully within. I never saw her for one instant in an attitude of what could have been taken as introspection, and I never heard her say anything that indicated reflection of any sort on the processes or contents of her mind.*

*It wasn't as though I missed anything like that from her, it had so early become so much a condition of her being that it really never crossed my mind that it could have been otherwise. But I understand now that she'd suffered in more than a trivial way from whatever had gone on with her and my father in those years when access to their relationship was forbidden to anyone else. I try to imagine during the last part of her life, after my father was gone, saying something to her about her anguish in her relations with him: I can see her face as I speak, and I can make out a subtle, all but imperceptible flinch strike her features; her mouth hardens, then reasserts itself, becomes as it was; she regards me not distantly, but from a place within herself of concealment. She isn't masked, really, but a quiet defiance has taken her, and I understand that if a memory of what may have hurt her did come loose within her for a moment, she's quickly soldered it back in place, and all I can hear her saying to me is something about what we're going to do today, what store to go to or movie to see. She's gone from me again then, as perhaps at some point in her time on earth, without ever realizing what was happening, she was gone from herself.*

Soon after I'd published my first book of poems, a psychologist friend of mine told me that he thought my father's secret desire had been to be a poet, and that I was enacting his wish for him. I was shocked, disagreed, but afterwards I had to admit there might be something to what he said; for one thing I was always a little puzzled about why I became a poet. For a long time I assumed that it was because being a poet was about the last thing that was expected of me, and surely that's partly true: I did want to define myself if not entirely as a rebel then at least as someone who hadn't accepted the norms and values of just about everyone I knew. I'd been telling my friend how my father would often read poetry to me when I was young, and would get me to memorize and recite poems to him; that my mother—though not he himself—had told me he'd been in a poetry club in high school, until he was expelled and sent on to another school—I always guessed it was because of a fight. I'd even once found what could have been called a poem scrawled on an envelope in his bureau when I was borrowing some socks. And what's more, though my mother may have been astonished—aghast—when I announced my intention to be a poet, my father didn't seem surprised at all. I'd been on an allowance for my expenses at college; when I graduated and told him I wanted to write, he continued to help me, though years passed before there was any sign that I'd accomplish anything.

Still, though I couldn't say I liked the idea of my life being dedicated to a dormant fancy of my father's, I had to recognize the justice of my friend's remark. My father had always seemed to have some expectation of me that I never quite understood. Although he made a cursory gesture of bringing me into his business, sending me out to sell machines that one summer, and having me work for a month another year at a machine making typewriter ribbons, tens of thousands of them, the most maddeningly tedious thing I ever did in my life, he never pushed me toward the business; the ribbon-making, if anything, seemed designed to drive me *away*. But even if he never said anything specific, he did always hint at other ambitions for me.

Now an odd thought, which is whether my father, rather than having had a real passion for poetry himself—he never opened a book of poetry after those first years of reading to me—might instead have been rather disinterestedly *experimenting* with me. I suppose that word might sound too cold, but aren't most parents involved in what might be defined as an experiment to see what kind of person their child-rearing will bring forth? No harm in that. And yet there's also the other word: *disinterestedly*, which implies a certain detachment, a lack of the fervor and the qualms parents are expected to feel about their offspring. I'm not quite sure why I use the term; perhaps it relates to the feeling I've had that at some point in our narrative together, long before he became apathetic toward life in general, my father became indifferent to me. I don't mean he became exasperated, all parents feel that. I'm hazarding something cooler, rather, something of which one would hesitate to accuse anyone.

I can't remember exactly when my father's disinterest would have revealed itself, perhaps when his business began to take more and more of his energy and to define his concentration so completely, but whenever it was, I understood, though I never allowed myself to acknowledge, that he really didn't care any longer what the general trajectory, or the details, or the outcome of my life might be. I didn't feel then there was any rancor about it; I'd just fallen from the field of matters with which he was seriously concerned.

And assuming that at least some variant of this was the case, mightn't there have been premonitions of it early on, alterations in the texture of his attention, that when I consider them now make me think that my existence became for him something very like an experiment?

This isn't a rhetorical question: I believe that it has to be answered definitely yes or no, or reformulated altogether. I'll try phrasing it this way: could my father have come to regard me and my outcomes more *objectively* than is generally expected of a parent? Although this skirts the issue of his interest or lack of it, perhaps the consequences are similar: in the short term perhaps, that kind of objectivity would have allowed for a more lively curiosity about the subject of one's experiment, a close scrutiny of its promise and realizations. But wouldn't such detachment also have effected a potentially more acute, because apparently objective, sense of disappointment, assuming one's experimental standards remained exacting, because the subject would, as subjects will, have wobbled a bit, bumped erratically into this wall or that, worked its way inefficiently through one's maze? Then the possibility of having to condition the subject would have arisen, of finding a way to make its maunderings more sensitive, more complex. All this also would have to have had a charge of dispassion in it: to arrive at such a decision would imply that the subject wasn't offering enough interest on its own, so why not expose it to the virus of one's old, discarded desires—poetry, in this case—to see what *that* might add to the equation? At some point, too, the necessity of having to deceive the poor thing would have arisen; finding a way to let it believe it was operating under its own system of choice, when in fact it was boiling away in a test tube.

Again, I may sound unkind here, but I don't mean to: I've had great pleasure in my inflictions, if I can call them that. Perhaps what I really mean to do is to endow my father in my memory with more self-consciousness than he would himself have had in generating the formulae he and I conspired in concocting, for after all, there had to have been something like a conspiracy to have made me what I am. I was certainly more recalcitrant than I've made it sound here; I must have presented a determined, erratic, disruptive detachment of my own. Any maze I was being put through must have resonated with my own assertions, and at times it would've been hard put to hold together when I rattled its walls with my rage for independence.

If my father was a thwarted or disabused poet, both he and my mother even perhaps more so were ruthless, all-but-professional critics. Everything that came into their ken had to be evaluated, measured, and judged. Everything. Anyone they met, every manifestation of the character of people they knew, every relationship, every thought, every act and emotion had to be defined as good or not good, useful or not useful, gratifying or irritating or intolerable, and on and on. They judged the appearance of their children: my father repeatedly told me to stand up straight, my mother fretted constantly about whether I was correctly dressed, adequately groomed, had a demeanor appropriate to the level of maturity she imagined was suitable for whatever age I was at the time. Sometimes it seemed they were most bound together when they were involved in a mutual assessment of someone or other. Perhaps that was why they seemed so severely to judge, both of them, the energy and industry of their children, our moral characters, our ethical virtues and flaws. (And of course when the conclusions they came to indicated faults or shortcomings, it was always implied that they'd had nothing to do with it.)

And, worst of all, I understand, alas, that I'm susceptible to such absurdities, too. I, too, seem to have to appraise, value, assess everything that happens around me, everything I do myself, every thought I have, every feeling, every act, and every act anyone else perpetrates in my ken, even those I love most. I have my mother's tendency to brood on causes, her passion to find reasons, and, though I don't like having to say so, her need to lay blame. From my father the urge to despise and dismiss anything that doesn't meet my expectations. Although, thank goodness, I've learned to keep my mouth shut most of the time, and my judgments seldom end in real contempt the way my father's so often did, or in the kind of hurt dissatisfaction my mother could communicate so well, this critical impulse feels like such an elemental part of my character that it becomes a serious question to me whether I absorbed it by having had it taught to me, by being in proximity to my parents for so long, or whether it might be something more basic, something in my genetic structure, or riding alongside it.

If this is the case, might it be not so much that I grew in many ways to be "like" my father and mother but rather that they and I are in all but the tiniest corner of our inherited halves essentially the same fragment of existence? And might that in turn mean that no matter how hard I try to distinguish myself from those qualities of my father that I loathed, and those of my mother that I tolerated only with impatience, I'm fated to repeat them? I think I've never used the term "fated" before and meant it.

"Don't kid a kidder," my father used to say sometimes when he suspected I might be telling him an untruth, or saying something only to gratify him. "Don't kid a kidder." It was meant to sound scornful, and it did, though it was less harsh than much else he inflicted on me, because at least it defined him as having perpetrated similar nonsense.

Is that what we were then, my father and I, two kidders kidding each other? To think such a thing might release me from any common fate we might share, not by evading it but by making me feel there's something nearly humorous and thus finally harmless and endearing about it all. Each of us the arguing halves of a single genetic propensity, so that rather than having been in conflict all that time we were just one another's ventriloquists: I open my mouth and out come his words; he opens his, and there are mine. I look into myself and find both of us, decked out in clown suits; trumpets and drums. My father, as amused as I am, peers out at me, perhaps accepting at last the gyrations the orchestra of our genes required from us.

About my mother, paradoxically, almost the opposite. There'd be no way to find our common inheritance humorous because she'd never have entertained the thought for a moment. She was resolutely serious: there was no question to her of "kidding," life was too solemn for that. I can't imagine her fooling around about anything crucial because she knew that if she did, someday she'd have to pay with an explanation, and then another, which would all be distractions, wasting moments that could better have been used for pleasure, or for concealing her pain from herself. Might I be like that, too? Don't I consider the ticks and tocks of my time with the same earnestness? Is this, too, predestined by my genes? Am I the same person my mother was, as well as my father? Shall I go with her even into her death, too, so we can enact the intricate chemical and psychic equation to which we're doomed? (Why, when I speculate about her, do I use the word "doom"? Was there at the base of her character a darkness, a realm unilluminated by any real hope for escape from her fearsome destiny?) I imagine the three of us fused in a cosmic entanglement. My mind careening through my memory right now: mightn't it be playing out an ancient necessity that generates the very cadences of the words I think? A solemn clown, a laughing puppet: how tell which? We don't choose any of this, do we? All we do is postulate grand terms to describe ourselves: necessity and chance, determinism and fate, love and . . . something else—or perhaps love and nothing but.

*I liked the house we lived in when we moved to the suburbs. It wasn't that much bigger than our old one, but was high on a hill overlooking the lights of a city in the distance, on a dead-end street: my mother, because of all the deaths by car she'd endured, had always wanted that. I liked, too, that there was a patch of tangled woods across from us, and that right next to the house, facing the breakfast room where we ate except when there was company, was a row of pine trees which on a dark night in warm weather with the windows open seemed in their tranquil immobility to become part of the room. In winter, when the window was closed and I could only see the glaring reflection of the family, I missed the trees, as though they'd been forbidden to me.*

*It was an agreeable place, but as soon as we moved there—I was fourteen—I began to sleep over at friends' houses as often as I could. It wasn't a conscious decision on my part; I just thought I liked sleeping at my friends' houses better than my own. I had a friend who lived a block away and one year I must have spent as many nights at his house as at my own. My parents didn't mind; I'd say I was going there to study, though mostly we watched television in my friend's room. The next year, a family with a* brother and sister about my age moved to town; I had a desperate, unrequited crush on the sister and liked the brother nearly as much, and I'd sleep at their house every night I could, but I overstayed my welcome: their mother, coming home from a vacation to find we'd had a party and had ruined her living room carpet, said to me in her anger: "Don't you have a home of your own?"

Did I? At the time, the most understanding I might have found in myself for my constant sleeping out would have had to do with my loneliness, because I always felt lonely then. Now I'd understand that the loneliness had to have come from somewhere, surely from what was going on then between my parents. My father during those years must have been doing exceptionally well at work, but he was often distracted with us, and had begun to act with an edge of something colder. At dinner sometimes he'd butter a piece of bread and toss it onto my plate, saying, "Eat," as though, literally, he were throwing me crumbs. And between him and my mother, I could sense new tensions. I have no precise notion of what disagreements they were having, or what fissures had opened between them; I only knew, without being quite aware of it, that there was a lot of tension between them, and that it affected me in a way I could never explain to myself. Later I came to think that those must have been the years when they were working out the truce in which they spent the last part of their lives. I still don't know how to specify it; you just knew there was no more intense attraction between them, that the essence of their being together now had to do with things and people and emotions other than and outside their former relationship. They weren't bitter enemies the way some couples are; there was just such an accumulation of misunderstandings and disappointments that they weren't passionate about each other anymore; perhaps the memory that they had once been that way added to the clench of unuttered anger I must have sensed between them. In their last years, in the next house they moved to, after I'd left home to live my own life, my mother would fall asleep every night watching television in the den; my father would go to bed, leaving her there, and he'd be gone in the morning before she got up. There were rarely unpleasant words between them; their arguments seemed petty, easily resolved; their social life was as active as ever; they were still a striking couple. But that was all.

At least until my mother said, "You used to be such a nice man," which had to be a violation of their unspoken pact. My father must have been as affronted by the transgression that sentence represented as he was by its content. Still, every time I used to think of her saying those words to him, I'd feel desolated. Even now, the summary judgments I can imagine being made about me have such a different flavor: "You're much more considerate than you used to be . . ." Or more clever, or sensitive, or, or, or . . . To have the compelling reversal inflicted upon you that my father did, even if it were true; how wounding it would be for me, how nearly mortal an accusation.

The years during which my father and mother evolved their sorrowful contract must have been confusing for me. No wonder I went to my friends: their houses seemed emotionally neutral, their parents incidental. How, at home, was I to find a space in myself for my parents' complex irreconcilabilities? Sometimes, if my friends were all busy, I'd take my sleeping bag and go out to spend the night in the backyard near those stolid, seemingly attentive pines.

It was in that same house, on the hill, not many years later, when my father for the first time made me think I might be his enemy, and he mine. There had been occasions before when he'd hurt me by the arbitrary way he'd exercise his authority over me; once, when I was going out on a date, he tried to forbid me from leaving the house. He had no reason, but, "Forget it," he said, "you're not going out." My mother intervened, though, and I did go. That sort of thing seemed rather trivial, a part of growing up, but the event I'm talking about now wasn't at all trivial; in tone, it seems to me to have been emblematic of all the years of wretchedness between my father and me.

It's dinnertime; we're all in the breakfast room. I don't live here anymore, I'm a year or so out of college, trying to learn to write, working all the time, reading, studying. My father, mother, brother, and sister are sitting at the table, for some reason I'm standing, leaning against the doorjamb; I think my arms are folded across my chest, perhaps in a rather confident way. I'm quite content for a change, I don't remember why: in those days I was almost always discouraged and displeased with myself, depressed and morose. Maybe it's because I'm home for a day or a night, escaped from the cave or cage where I believe I'm trying to teach myself discipline. Maybe my writing has been going well, though it rarely did then. Everyone else seems in a good mood, too; there's laughter, I'm enjoying the welcoming texture of family and of that room—it really was a nice place to be.

I'm talking just now about my work, when I mention how many books I have to buy because I read them so quickly, my father says something about my spending too much money on books, and I lift my hand toward him in what I thought and still think was an ordinary gesture of dispute or dissension. I say something in return, not with ill feeling, certainly not in anger, just with a joking argumentativeness, something like, "If I don't read books, I might as well forget about being a writer," and suddenly, so suddenly, *Don't shake your finger at me!* my father . . . *snarls,* I suppose would describe the ferocity of his voice, his malevolence, his apparent abhorrence of me. He says it not as one would speak to one's offspring, not to anyone else in a family, to an employee, even to a stranger. Perhaps to an enemy one has bested, or the subject of an interrogation.

When I was very young, one or the other of my parents would often say to me, when I'd try to argue with them, "Don't contradict." This was presented not as the constituent stage of a debate which was about to come to a conclusion, but as a rhetorical absolute: do not utter anything in opposition to what one of your parents is saying to you, no matter how self-evident the truth you're trying to express might be. I always had to acknowledge their superior authority, and I'd submit. But I never understood, why not contradict? Even then I believed that human communication presumes, surely, an equality of intention: you speak, I understand; I speak, you try to understand as well. But no: there was this barrier of sheer force, this limit, this beyond which not.

My father, now, though, seems to be assaulting me, threatening, menacing, his teeth almost bared in rage, all of which I know can't have anything to do with what I've been saying to him, nothing to do with what we've been chatting about, nothing in content, certainly nothing in mood. My father is saying something as authoritarian as that long gone, much gentler precept about contradiction, but this time his purpose isn't to stop the quibbling of a child who probably wants something he shouldn't have anyway, nor is it to teach a point of etiquette, nor to shut down an argument because one's son has reached the stage of understanding that there can be no conclusive resolution to a discussion as long as he can keep shifting its terms.

What is his point, then? Is there one? I've never seen him quite like this, and I don't yet suspect how often from then on I will. All of us are shocked. I can still feel the tears that almost came to my eyes, tears of shame and resentment, but I'd already by then contrived to render my tear ducts inoperative and to control absolutely my sensitivity to shock—even a firecracker someone once set off under my chair when I was playing the piano couldn't make me flinch. So the tears don't reach my eyes; I keep them farther away, farther within, though I'm no less jarred by my father's vehemence: I have no idea, at least not yet, how to respond to such rancor, such venom, such apparent enmity.

Why is he being like this? Is there something about me he suddenly finds intolerable? "Suddenly" hardly captures the abruptness of his turning on me. Do I think, how can I not think, that he's been waiting for this, for the chance to express his animosity, his execration of me? Waiting how long? Might this be really about money? Because I take money from him? I take hardly anything then; I live in one room, I dress and eat simply, I hardly drink alcohol; I aspire to asceticism; the young artist as adept, devotee.

If it's not money, then, might it be something worse? Have I been laboring to create an identity that my father will find repugnant? *Does* find repugnant, already, though I'm painfully conscious of how unformed, how incomplete I still am?

My mother looks as taken aback as I am. Like any child of any family, I sometimes try to set one parent against another; there'll be a time not much later when it will seem to me that any conflict has ultimately to be decided by how a woman views it: always a woman, always, I'll know even then, the mother. But not now: there's no chance for that now, this has happened too quickly, there's no time here for questions of rightness, of justice. My mind races to find what was the trigger for this, the snap of the bolt. I can tell my mother's mind is racing like mine, and for an instant I feel a feather of pity for her, because I can tell she's hurt, too, and is as uncomprehending as I am. My parents aren't yet at the stage where she might tell my father he's no longer a nice man. She just looks at him in silence, or not at him, toward him rather; I don't think her eyes ever reach him, as though she doesn't yet quite believe that the words came from him. Her eyes, whatever she might wish them to do, stop short of him, so that she seems to be, no, surely is, looking out the window at those trees. But I can't look away: I just stare at my father, who stares back, still with venom, still with execration. His face is almost as distorted as it was on those evenings of my childhood when we would play together, when he'd hunch himself like a great spider, explode the tendons in his neck, and reveal to me his mask of mock-murderousness.

What ends this now? Someone must get up and say, Let's go in the den. Or, Who wants coffee? Or, or, or. Someone has to say something; all I know is what's not being said: *What's happening to us? Will all this rage, this pain, this sorrow heal? Ever? If not, will it be accounted for? How? By whom?*

When I told my father I didn't want to
take money from him anymore, he answered, "If you don't take it, the tax man
will." We were in his car, he was in an especially good mood, so was I, and we must
have both been pleased to be free for a
time from whatever was boiling between
us in those years. He was alert, attentive to
what I said, not detached or preoccupied as
he usually was even when we were alone
together, and I felt close to him. Telling
him I thought the money should stop
was a part of that feeling of closeness; it
was also a confession, perhaps, or a plea:
maybe I wanted reassurance that my taking
money from him wasn't the reason for his
distorting what had once been our love for
one another, a love which so often now
was more like a curse. I told him I thought
it wasn't doing either of us any good for
me to keep accepting his money but he
just said that it was there, he couldn't use it
all, and that it was ridiculous to let it go to
waste. Then he changed the subject.

And I gave in. If that's what the term
should be, because of course I still did
want the money I'd taken from my father

all those years because, I told myself, it gave me time to write—I only had to teach one semester a year now instead of two—and surely that was the case, but even so: who can't use extra money? I accepted his reasoning, maybe I'd known all along, or hoped it was what he'd say, but I realize now that our transactions couldn't have been as neutral as he made them out to be that day, there had to have been murkier depths; he didn't know himself, or me, nearly as well as he thought he did.

My father was extraordinarily generous. He gave money to me and my brother and sister. He helped establish various relatives in their professions and businesses, with loans and gifts. At the end of his life, he was sending money every month to a university student he said was the son of some distant relative I'd barely heard of, and after he died, I found in his letters an exchange he'd had with the warden of a federal prison in another state, and thus I discovered I still had a first cousin, from one of my father's brothers' first, almost-obliterated-from-memory marriage, whom I hadn't seen since I was three or four years old, whom I'd completely forgotten about and who, at the time my father wrote, was in a penitentiary, serving a long sentence, for a not unserious offense. My father had written the warden proposing that if his nephew were paroled, my father would give him a job. The warden wrote back saying that there was absolutely no chance of this prisoner being paroled; he was violent, a troublemaker, a career criminal, and he'd probably spend the rest of his life in prison. (I've learned recently that he hasn't.)

Again, soon after my father died my mother received the newsletter of a church from a small town in another state. The pastor had written to his congregation that he'd heard about my father's death, and he wanted to tell them how, as a young man, he'd been working as a caddie at the club where my father played golf, and my father had sensed his dissatisfaction, and had offered him a more interesting, higher-paying job in his printing business, which pleased the minister no end. Then, just after he'd started work, he'd carelessly put an essential freight elevator out of commission. He was mortified, but my father had treated him with what the pastor said was an inspiring trust and loyalty that had helped the future pastor, he wrote now, understand the real meaning of Christian charity. And, he concluded, my father wasn't a Christian at all, but a Jew!

My father loved doing things like that. Sometimes, as I've said, it was because he liked the effect as much as the gesture. When he decided that he didn't want to work in his original branch office anymore, instead of putting it up for sale, he ran an ad in *The Wall Street Journal* offering to *give* the business away if he could find the right person. He received a deluge of responses, interviewed a lot of applicants, but for whatever reason he never found anyone he had confidence in—or maybe no one who appreciated the sheer theater of what he was doing—so he sold the branch after all.

Still, giving the chauffeur a chance to become a truck driver and acquire some dignity, teaching the repairman to become a salesman, helping out relatives and sometimes friends: it all wasn't done for show. Always when he helped someone, he'd take particular satisfaction in not expecting anything in return.

Except from his children. This is hard: I have no desire to appear thankless for all my father gave me, and for the freedom it allowed me to live the life I have. I'll always be grateful for that. In that conversation just before he died, when my father spoke of us being kids together, he also told me how proud he was of my career as a poet. I replied that I couldn't have done it without him, and he answered, Don't be silly. Don't kid a kidder. But I wasn't just being sentimental at a sentimental moment, perhaps the most touching moment my father and I ever had together: I meant it, at least partly. Though I know what I said wasn't literally true, the feeling I meant to convey by it was; I wanted my father to know that despite everything, he'd shared in my life in a way that meant a great deal to me.

Why, then, this expression of qualification, of compunction? My father gave me money and he never overtly asked for anything in return. How even begin to speak of money and feelings? Money has such an excessive, savage hold on the spirit, of those who have it and those who don't, of those who give it and those who take. We call money a symbol, but that drastically understates the intricate interweavings it has with our regard for others, our self-regard, and with how it tangles our hearts in its ropy, tenacious tendrils.

*There was a paper-cutting machine in my father's printing plant: it was like a huge electric guillotine, with a heavy press that descended to hold the stacks of paper on its steel table, and a blade that sliced viciously down, with an excruciating sound. One day, during a school vacation, I went to the plant with my father; there was an important printing job to be finished and my father himself—still in his business suit—began to operate that horrific machine. I was terrified he was going to maim himself: I felt the same anxiety you do watching someone dancing on the edge of a roof, an almost intolerable, almost physically nauseating dismay as his hands moved in and out of that appalling contraption. One doesn't have to be a psychologist to interpret the layers of dread I felt, the misplaced aggressions tearing at me. Thinking about it now, I realize I was often afraid for my father; not in situations as obvious as this: I was troubled mostly about what might happen to him if his reality ever ceased reinforcing his sense of himself as effective, potent, successful.*

*My sophomore year in high school, just after our family moved to the suburbs, our English class was assigned to read a book by William Dean Howells,* The Rise of Silas Lapham.

*Although the title implies the success of the protagonist, in fact the story is more about his failure, about how he loses the fortune he'd made only a short time before, and how through no fault of his own, no flaw, no hubris, his life unravels and all he's come to value is taken from him. I've often wondered why we would have been given a book with such a grim vision of business or commerce, a life most of us assumed we'd end up in. For whatever reason, perhaps because of our teacher's resentment of the prosperous, spoiled children we were, with our cashmere sweaters and cars, that book might very well have been meant to inculcate a sense of insecurity in us: we were to take from it the idea that what destiny holds for us is always potentially tragic. And it wasn't just that one book; much of our culture then, not long after the Depression, consisted of cautionary tales designed to warn us that failure is always lurking in success, that if we weren't vigilant and properly humble we well might be cast down, like Lapham, or Willy Loman, or even the great Lear. And wasn't Loman a salesman just as my father had been and in some ways still was? Wouldn't it have taken just the slightest suspension of good fortune or of my father's energy for us to have ended up like Loman's blighted family, beset with disappointment and regret?*

*It would happen, too, that some of my parents' friends did, like characters in fiction, lose everything, have to sell their houses and possessions; I noticed my parents would speak the people's names in something like whispers, then after a short while I wouldn't hear about them at all, but I'd wonder what had become of them, how their spirits had survived their ruin. And I'd quake to think of my father subjected to such ravaging misfortune. Maybe at the end, when it was clear he was going to get out of his life without being disgraced, I felt a kind of re-*

lief. *A few years after he died, one of the two businesses that were left went into bankruptcy, then failed completely, and the other came close to folding, as well. My first thought was to be thankful that my father didn't have to experience such disaster.*

Yet, even now, so many years later, I can't
help remembering how much my father
could take from you as a reparation for
his munificence, and how infuriatingly des-
potic he could be about it. He'd tell you,
for instance, he'd *promise* he was going to
do something for you—loan you money
to help with the down payment on a
house, say, as he did with my sister—and
when you tried to remind him of it, he'd
act, no, he *might* act, which in some ways
made it even harder, as though he'd never
said anything of the sort. Things like that
didn't happen only near the end of his life
when in his depression he might really
have forgotten what he'd said, he was always prone to it, and of course the reasons
were much more complex than his having
forgotten what he'd agreed to. It seemed as
if you asked him for something before he
offered it, or even reminded him of a favor
he'd already offered, he'd think you were
trying to best him, or cheat him—I don't
know what, really. All you knew was that
you'd feel humiliated and impotent; the
only appropriate response seemed to be
throw a tantrum like a child, "But you

promised!" which of course you weren't about to do. What you were going to do was to rage in silence, or, like my sister, write a dozen-page letter telling him what he'd done and how it had hurt you. During the worst years, though, nothing you could say mattered to him.

Once I told him to keep his fucking money. We were on the phone, he was threatening to cut me off, because he thought I'd talked my brother into separating from his first wife, soon after I'd separated from mine. I'd done nothing of the sort, but my father wouldn't believe me, and kept at me and at me until finally I said it: Keep your fucking money! And meant it: I was more enraged than he was, I was sick to death of money getting into everything, infecting everything: I was tired all at once of my acquiescence, my weakness, my having consented to disregard so much of what I felt.

By the time we saw each other again, we'd both calmed down, and neither of us brought up what I'd said. I suppose I was relieved, but perhaps disappointed as well; I must have realized that things would have been better between us without that complication, and, at least in some ways, he must have thought so, too. Sometimes I've wondered why he didn't take me up on what I'd said. Might he have been afraid that if he stopped giving me money, he'd lose control over me? Yet he never tried to dictate the way I lived, even though he may well have objected to it. Maybe he was addicted to the tension between us, that strumming sometimes of love, sometimes of anything but love. If I had turned my back on his money, he would, yes, have had to let go of a part of the link between us. Sometimes in his most bitter moods there seemed to be nothing he wanted more than just that, as though his real desire was to alienate me altogether. Might those times when he was so perversely cruel have had their origins in those obscure confusions? Was this how so much that was vile and pointless could have come out of him, so much that left me to speculate, feverishly, in the way of my mother, on the reasons for his animosity, because if I could uncover those reasons then I'd be able, again like my mother, to *blame*; blame him, the crass culture of money that conditioned him, the moral mistrust that possessed him.

With all that, though, I understand now how bereft my father would have been without me, how diminished. And I realize, too, how much I'd have sacrificed if I'd had to give up my connection to him.

The first time he was in the hospital for any length of time, to have a detached retina repaired, he became frightened that he might end up completely blind, and money came up again. The operation hadn't worked, had to be done once more, then still again. He had bandages over his eyes for more than a week, had to be fed and taken to the bathroom, and naturally hated what was happening to him. When I was visiting him one afternoon, he said to me that maybe he wouldn't be able to help us all anymore, that he might have to stop working. I realized that by saying this, by trying to lighten the extent of his concerns, he was trying to diminish his terror of going blind, and I said, probably with relief, Fine, don't worry about it. I had a part-time, badly paid job then, but I knew I'd be able to find something. What else, though, might what he said have implied? Apparently, not giving me money would have had symbolism for him, as much as giving it. What, though? Sometimes it can seem the logic for all of this is as much metaphysical as psychological.

In the end, he recovered from the operations, went back to his businesses, and nothing changed. Nothing changed: we still struggled, still fought, still lied. Because though my father believed he never asked anything in return for what he gave me, in truth he asked much. He asked without quite knowing what he asked, and without quite knowing, either, I tried, dutifully, fervently, to give him what he wanted. The trouble was, the source of our common frustration was that he never articulated and possibly, probably, never knew what he wanted from me. There were periods when we pretended we were both satisfied with the protocols of our contract, and I know we thought then we were, but always it would begin again: his unspoken, perhaps unwitting demands, my attempts, conscious and unconscious, to satisfy them. It's impossible to describe how all those complexities were expressed. Not, or not completely, by our words, not by our gestures, not even as a covert footnote to what we were with each other. A mood? More than that. A condition of being, like pores that sweat, glands that secrete, nerves that shudder? Less than that. Our misunderstandings were precariously balanced between us, and we responded to each other like the strings of a musical instrument set trembling by another instrument being plucked.

*My father's suffering when he was dying was awful, for him and for all of us. Not the physical aspect of it; he seemed long since to have almost completely overcome the necessity to acknowledge his body's anguish, except in the most extreme circumstances. When I was an adolescent, he once took me to the dentist with him. The dentist was going to do some serious drilling, and asked my father if he wanted Novocain; my father said, No, go ahead. The dentist began, and a moment later stopped. Are you sure you don't want something? he asked. My father shook his head; the dentist, clearly troubled, began to drill again, then paused to look at my father as if to ask the same question again, but my father made no sign, so he went on. Afterwards I asked my father whether it hadn't hurt. "I have a high threshold of pain," he said. I suspect he may have been showing off for me, or that he was trying to teach me something, but if it was to be able to bear pain as he had, the lesson was beyond me.*

*I saw something like that again, near the end, when he was in the hospital for an absolutely unnecessary biopsy on his brain. The whole time, with everything else that was going on, he complained that his arm hurt. Finally, an* orthopedic specialist was sent to examine him. He must have assumed nothing was seriously wrong: he poked at the arm, then held his hand to my father's and told my father to push as hard as he could. My father pushed back against the doctor's hand, grimacing horribly, until the doctor told him to stop, then, ashen, he fell back. It was only then that the doctor went out—I followed without him knowing it—to speak to the attending intern. They looked at an X-ray of the arm, and, "Didn't you see this?" the orthopedist asked, showing the intern that there was a tumor in the bone of the biceps, and a long crack. But this was after he'd "examined" my father. Later, I happened to see another X-ray of the arm taken just before my father was discharged: there was a clear fracture now, the bone had broken and the ends had moved about half an inch from each other, and I realized that because of those quacks, and because of how he could tolerate pain, my father had broken his own arm.

He had a great deal of physical discomfort in his life. He had a chronically bad back, and his arthritic knees caused him, especially toward the end, much distress; his eyes became worse and worse, so by the time he died he could barely see. He'd had bad eyesight from childhood, and in late middle age he had those operations for his detached retinas, but he had inoperable cataracts which kept the retinas from ever being properly treated. By the end he couldn't read and could hardly make out images on television, which rendered the empty hours of his ruminating on his disintegration all the bleaker. Still, though, when he'd get up from a chair and sometimes groan, I often felt it wasn't because of the pain itself, but because he wanted us to know about and acknowledge it.

But it was his spiritual suffering, if I can call it that, against which he seemed to have no defense. He was very susceptible in his last years to depression, although the term barely conveys the all-encompassing fullness of his despair. Frightening it would be to call him on the phone and have his stricken, droning, seemingly half-paralyzed voice come back to you. You knew that anything you had to say to him was being heard only by the shell containing him; there was an unbridgeable distance between his real inner life and the person to whom you believed you were speaking. A void, negation, despair: I'd feel so much dread having to hear him in his sadness that I was relieved when my mother would answer the phone and I could send greetings without having to speak to him. When I did, he sounded so engulfed by his misery, there was so much irrationality hovering at the edges of what he'd say, that I felt he might do something to harm himself; sometimes I thought he'd already irrevocably harmed himself, at least in his soul.

I've often wondered about my father's soul, about the cosmos in which he dwelt. What were the ultimate grounds of his beliefs, of his day-to-day confrontations with existence? What meaning did life have for him? Did he believe in a real God? How much had being a Jew in the century of Jewish horror affected him? We never spoke about that, or never seriously: surely it would have had to affect him to realize that it was the purest chance that his and my mother's grandparents had left Poland and Russia when they did, and so it was just as much a chance that he was still alive at all. If he felt anything like that, though, he kept it to himself, as most Jews of his generation did.

But surely he was "religious": when his own father died, he went to synagogue every morning for a year to say Kaddish, no matter where he was, and then he kept going, so that for the last twenty years or so of his life he presumably prayed every day. But of what did his prayer consist? During his last days, when all he wanted was to have his partial life over with, the word "God" never came up, just as the word "death" didn't later with my mother. And yet if he could have, I know my father would have kept going to synagogue right to the end. He especially loved the more Orthodox shuls, where old men wrapped in their prayer shawls muttered and swayed. My father wore a tallis, too, and a yarmulke, and read Hebrew quite well, but I still wonder: did he have a God?

Perhaps he had to, but if so, I don't believe he found any consolation in his belief. So much of his intellectual and emotional structure had to do with his determination, his will; and the way the will works, by a constant process of assessment, correction, and redirection, then action and self-chastisement if that action isn't successful, implies a turn against the self, the necessity constantly to confront self and compel it to a higher state. Yet what if someone's conception of that higher state becomes detached from any realistic vision of the self's capacities? What, in other words, if the demands of the will outstrip its means? What consoles then?

Finally my father seemed to believe that
he'd constructed himself as an instrument
of his own resolve; maybe that's what happens to people who succeed in the world
by what they interpret as force of character. But the self is more complex and more
vulnerable than that; the self my father
made was overwhelmed in the end by the
enormity of his unacknowledged and perhaps unfelt longings, and by the shadow-
ings of an ennui he never understood.

His God in those last, hard years I
imagine as the pure function of his struggle with himself, which must be what gods
most often are. And yet it seems to me that
the only means by which my father would
seem to have been able to approach his
God was by yet another act of will, or by a
suppression of his will by itself: you can't
will a God into your presence, such a God
would be unworthy of you; what's left is to
find a way to have God disclose Himself to
you by redefining yourself, by creating a
self whose resolve would be subservient to
some other purpose, a self that won't have
to be so relentlessly muscular, so flexed before life and the cosmos.

Perhaps my father did sometimes achieve a relation of that sort with his God. I picture him in the synagogue, praying: he certainly looks sincere, devoted, involved. And he did, in his own terms, sometimes turn the force of his determination to religious ends. Yom Kippur, the Day of Atonement and fasting, I always believed was his favorite day of the year, because then his will could work as efficiently and selflessly as it had in the dentist's chair. There was never any question of him eating, or drinking, or smoking, or brushing his teeth on Yom Kippur, the way everyone else I knew did, because on that day his purposes and what his God asked of him were perfectly in accord: You demand this of me, and without compunction, without evasion, I obey You.

But what of all the other days, the other hours of those days, the other moments? Hearing his voice when he was in his void of despair, you heard the echo of those dark hours which had expanded and harrowingly inhabited him now. Would he have ever blamed God for such suffering? Could someone like him say to his God that the God lacked anything? Might he have blamed his God for the slaughter of so many in the Shoah? He never hinted at anything like that, perhaps it never occurred to him, or perhaps it was something so deep in him that he never bothered to articulate it, or could.

And did he ever, my father, imagine that *he* lacked something, spiritually, in the capacity of his soul, in the configuration of the consciousness in which he existed? Did the Day of Atonement ever actually mean atonement, and hence change, rather than the will accomplishing itself in ritual? Someone who swears never again to say they're sorry, even to sons, even to a wife: can that person be capable of repenting, even to a God, possibly repudiating his own ethic before the entity he most respects, perhaps the only entity he truly respects?

I like to think that at some point toward the end my father had an argument like this with himself, however inarticulately. His death, when he finally attained it, was wonderfully serene. Although so many of his feelings about dying apparently had to do with his relief at being set free from the absurdity of his aphasia, and escaping from his repellent body, there was something beyond that; an acceptance, even a sweetness, that made me think that perhaps he had turned to his God in such a way that the wounds of his will had been annealed. He looked peacefully asleep when I came into the room after he'd died. His eyes were a little open. I closed them, surprised, despite myself, that he'd let me close them, that he didn't protest, and surprised, too, I think, that they stayed closed.

*My father has been dead a long time, my mother a brief ten years less. I imagine them now side by side, in their coffins, in their graves. Strange to visualize all the couples under the tireless lid of the earth, sledding on their backs together through space and time, always as though patiently waiting to move toward one another, to come together again or at last, as though to begin another journey.*

*I imagine that my mother lying there is still a little tense, as she was when she fell asleep in front of the television or reading: she'd be caught nearly upright against the back of the sofa, her face not decontracted in sleep, but scowling a little, as though she'd been surprised by unconsciousness and was waiting protestingly to wake again to go into her other bed, her other sleep, beside my father.*

*Now I picture my father next to her, resolutely unmoving, plunged again into the forceful stillness which always had defined his not being awake. Willfully inattentive, willfully inaccessible I see him, perhaps so nothing again can be said to him about his not being something or being something; all that had long ceased to interest him. When he died, it was as though he moved into a real sleep for the first* time; he seemed to release himself from the responsibility of being himself; he was simplified, and, except for the traces of the physical suffering that still marked him, he looked as if he earnestly wanted to convey how it was to be so much at peace.

I see them there, and still I wonder if when the time should arrive for them to come together whether my mother will be released, too, from her resentment and unease, and be able to reach a hand across to my father as she hadn't for so many years, to move closer, to partake of his space with him, of the solace of that real proximity which had been forbidden to her for all that time by no one can remember what. And my father: would he release himself from the rigors of his oblivion to acknowledge my mother, to accept her hand upon him, her breast against him, to sway, even just a little, even across that so slight space which would connect them to one another again, like lovers again, like young husband and wife, not like combatants, negotiators of a truce that never achieved real disarmament or peace?

I imagine them in the unrelenting nearness of their solitudes, in their eternity of grief for themselves, and suddenly the thought comes to me, with so much of a shock that I almost say it aloud: But they loved each other! I feel almost embarrassed to think such an obvious thought, and yet I think it again: They loved each other all along, perhaps not always, and perhaps not every moment, they were in love!

Under certain circumstances they were in love, I think then: when certain conditions had been met, when various compromises were in effect, and effective. And I wonder how a state of emotion like love can be characterized as so straitened, so contained? Don't you trivialize love by conceiving of it as taking place under the weight of circumstances and conditions and compromises?

*But how still more demeaning to think of love excluding concessions and restrictions. What love, even the most apparently fulfilled, the most passionate and solicitous and tender, doesn't begin at its very conception to procreate conditions? What love doesn't demand unstated contracts of consent and compulsion, which must be taught and learned; sensitivities which must be cultivated, as gently and as patiently as possible, but hurriedly, ineptly, if need be, so as to allay the fears any soul feels in bestowing its vulnerabilities upon another?*

*Is there any love that doesn't ask of the loved one recognition and submission to exigencies that can never precisely match the exigencies of the other because then there would be no other, only a multiplied self?*

*I see my father and mother in their graves and I understand that when they were alive, she asleep on her sofa and he sprawled in his weary bed, they were expressing the love that they had to express, which they had chosen to dwell in, which they meant to dwell in and express, however they arrived at their accord.*

They loved each other! *I think again, and wonder again: Is any love to be judged? Is any love to be measured according to the greater or lesser number of exceptions it entails? If two people love in what looks to a third like a maze of qualms and qualifications, does it disentitle their love? Or might the observer reveal his or her own limitations by thinking such a thought?*

*Is love to be judged at all, as good or bad, rich or distorted, healthy or maimed?*

*And the conditions one has made oneself and the needs one has fulfilled to satisfy one's own definition of love, one's own offering to the beloved one has found to be worthy, and necessary: is anyone ever sufficiently conscious of themselves to know how they've shaped the love they experience so that it* can be presented to themselves and the beloved as ineluctably worthy?

We learn early on that there are questions we can ask about love, and of love, and that other questions are forbidden; perhaps that's what brings us to think that love precludes questioning, although we know that it boils with questions and quandaries. And yet at the end doesn't love deal rather gently with us? For love, the seeming contradictions between good and bad, true and false, beautiful and not beautiful, aren't nearly as important as they are for other voyages of the psyche. Love gives us the right to hold contradictory judgments, about ourselves, about the ones we love: we discover truths that would be in absurd opposition if they hadn't been spun in love's loom.

My mother and father loved one another when they were with others, when my father smiled his ingenuous smile that revealed the imperfection of his teeth, the accent mark of his delight. Then my mother's smile, too, would brighten, become open, affirm their to her still astonishing union. They loved one another when they danced; as they held each other and beamed in pride and perhaps in an abiding wonder at themselves. My father no longer limped, my mother no longer was in bondage to her anxieties and her ambitions, even her physical self was at ease, suddenly lighter, released into the quickened tempi of her pleasure. They were in love even when they were alone, turned away from each other, in silence, with no one to behold them, no one to remark their assertions or refutations.

I imagine them again under the earth, perhaps no longer waiting for anything now but content to be as they are, bound in their imperfect but everlasting devotion, gliding through the first lobe of their eternity together.

After her death, after I told my mother, my mother's withered, tormented body, that I loved her, I sobbed, dryly, painfully, three times, four, in a tone and from a region of my voice I'd never known were there. I said again, "I love you," and stroked her face. The sound of her breathing all those last days, every gasp of air in, every reluctant exhalation, seemed to echo in the room, amplifying her stillness and silence. How much she wanted to stay with us.

And she wouldn't have been able to know, because she would have thought it terrifying, cosmically threatening to know she was dead, how much, once dead, she would stay with us, within us. I hear her voice even as I wait there with her for whatever in me will tell me when I can leave her; I hear her voice now as it called me those nights across the spaces of my being into my sleep. That voice of reassurance that must have had so arduous a coming through the mufflings of her anxiety, and yet which had come, with so much self-abnegation, bringing its lucid and solacing pronouncements of attentiveness and affection.

"Leave her": such a shocking thing to think. Isn't it she who's left me? That day so long ago comes to me again when she took me to school to put me in its charge, to give me away, I surely felt. We're in the school office, her hands grip the edge of the counter, and she's leaning forward, speaking urgently. She tells the person to whom she's speaking what she's told me, that I'm too intelligent not to be in school, even if I am technically too young. She looks at the person shyly, but intently, and her body expresses her anxiety, subtle, but clear, a desperate asservation. The woman to whom she speaks, pleads, must sense the urgency of her distress, and perhaps senses, too, my unqualified commitment to do anything, sacrifice anything to please my mother, so I'm admitted to kindergarten. Then my mother and I walk out of the school together; she's relieved and delighted, I'm delighted for her. Her red hair, of which I'm aware already she's so proud, strikes a swath of color across the dim gray stone of the school building where I'll spend so many lonely days. I'm entirely happy for her, and if I feel any concern about leaving her to enter the classroom, I pay it no mind; it's enough to be there this moment, watching her, that's all I need, all I ask from her, from my mother.

Who lies before me now, aslant on the narrow bed of her struggle with death. The nurse has removed the intravenous tubes and rearranged the turban the poor bald cancer patients wear, but I take it off so I can see and touch her head again, that just-revealed childlike roundness, the soft new hair. I become ever more conscious of how weary I am, of how grueling the half week of her dying and the half year of her illness have been. I think to myself that I'll find a way later when I'm less drained to say a fuller goodbye to her; someday I'll tell her in my mind how I miss her, someday I'll thank her for how much of herself she risked to have divided herself when she was so young, so unprepared, so vulnerable, into the double creature she and I were those first years, and the linked beings we always would be.

I see her again now: we're in a playground, I'm still small enough for her to lift me and set me on the seat at one end of a seesaw. Then she sits on the other end, delicately, as though she weighed as little as I do, and levers me gently into the sky, from whence, ecstatic, amazed, I look down at her, and at the world around her. Now that room again, she and I, the wash of light becoming golden as I intently, hiddenly watch her comb her hair.

. . . Which along with everything else about her is already only a fragment of memory now, or perhaps not only; perhaps really we complete those we love, fulfill their finally unchanging essence, when they're gone from us, when we take into ourselves those portions of them still available to us, to acknowledge them more perfectly, more purely, and do homage to the fugitive, protean forms of love of, and love from.

When I touch my father after his death, when I close his eyes, stroke his face, something shudders in my chest, I reel within myself for a moment, all the muscles of my own face seem to harden, I can think of nothing more to say to him than I've already choked out about our war, though I know there's much I would say if I could. Then it occurs to me that this silence, half-mind, half-body, that's taken me is grief, and I feel that perhaps I'm honoring my father in the one currency that would still have value to him, my anguish for him, my mourning not for having lost him, for he's still here in my emotions and still before me in his flesh, but because I've lost that aspect of him, his existence, the sheer fact of his being, all I'd always kept with me as I blundered through my life.

To my mother I say, "I love you," to my father I speak of war; yet aren't both declarations after all of attachment and allegiance?

My father's glasses are off. Except when he was young, and would take them off for his picture to be taken, he always wore them, and always seemed to me unlike himself without them. When I was a child and he'd pretend he was going to wrestle with me, crush me, he'd take his glasses off first, and even before he went into his dance of menace he was already unrecognizable and forbidding. Now, though, without them he seems more himself than he's ever been, even during those last days when he knew he was going and had fiercely reaffirmed his proprietary rights over himself.

I wonder again whether my father would have heard me say what I said, the way my mother, far, far away in her coma, may have heard my aunt. Would he have understood me, and realized why what came to me were words of a recognition neither of us had ever spoken?

Forgiveness is such an elusive act. Why, when we're at last prepared to relinquish our estrangements, when we've all but forgotten the grounds for our disapprobation and are ready at last to speak of the incomprehension that surged through us unsaid, does there seem nothing to be said, and, at the end, nothing to forgive? We seem suddenly to have neither the need nor the right to forgive; the very concept of forgiveness can feel repellent and debasing.

And why, too, once having realized and enacted our forgiveness as well as we can, do we at once seem forgiven ourselves, so that sometimes we can mistrust in ourselves our reasons for having forgiven: might our being shriven of blame ourselves be all we really were after? But perhaps forgiveness is a process more than an emotion, perhaps it's meant to make us discover those other conditions within ourselves, love, belief in love, to which forgiveness itself is incidental: perhaps forgive-

ness once accomplished becomes a condition of existence, a reality as ineluctable as our physical and mental
being.

My father and I are silent now. The silence between parent and child, the whir through us of old
emotions, the tangled chords of our misunderstandings,
the chaotic scraps of never pronounced phrases of explanation and intention: I feel nothing of that.

In the days and weeks and months after my father
dies, I'll dream about him often, more than I'd have
thought. My mother, when she dies, will take a long
time to come to my dreams; when she finally appears
it'll be in the most matter-of-fact way, with no fuss at
all; she often seems to be smiling at me out of my
dream.

But in the first dreams I have of my father, he
doesn't seem to know quite where he is; I can sense a
lack of assurance in him, a diffidence: he doesn't seem
unhappy, but he's terribly uncertain. Often he seems to
want to say something to me, but he never can state
whatever it is clearly enough for me to understand. As
time passes, I have dreams in which he begins to seem
alert, content, self-possessed; he's always very involved
in what's going on in the dream: when there's a task to
be performed, he helps me with it, always in a very un-
obtrusive way. Then come dreams in which he seems
utterly at peace with himself; he moves easily into and
through dreams, and comes and goes from them calmly,
and his being in a dream and his departure from it are
both so unpretentious and guileless that I'm comforted,
and released, I'm not sure why, from an apprehension of
my own, perhaps from my abiding desire to be other

than I am. And that feeling of acceptance stays with me even when I wake; sometimes I think it might be the last gift my father bestowed on me.

Now, waiting next to his body, perhaps I have a premonition of that gift; perhaps I sense that the resignation and serenity of the time before my father's dying has passed on to me, although I don't know yet how all of it will be manifested in me, or when.

What I do now is lift my father's arm, the one that hadn't been broken: it weighs so much, feels so inert, yet it expresses not loss, not incompletion, but a reassuring finality. It makes me feel not as though my father has evaded his real death, escaped his body's destruction and his mind's terror of debility, but as though he's arrived at the state of being he'd set out for from the beginning. I think that perhaps his will has conquered his complexities at last, and his death has brought a fruition he'd never imagined to his will.

I hear my mother in the other room as the rest of the family tries to comfort her. She doesn't really believe yet my father is dead, though she's been told. Someone has said, "It's over," but she hasn't really understood. Now she comes in, looks for a moment with almost no expression at my father, then lies down next to him, adjacent to but not quite touching him, and her eyes close. I watch them both, my mother and father, I watch myself watching, then I go.

Printed in the USA
CPSIA information can be obtained
at www.ICGtesting.com
LVHW091134150724
785511LV00001B/135